BE-You-TIFUL

THE THREEFOLD PROCESS
TO BECOMING YOU

JADA COLLINS

Jada Collins Publishing

For more information, please contact:

jadacollinsonline.com

Book and Cover Design:

Arbor Books, Inc.
www.arborbooks.com

Cover Photography: Bruce Talbot
Makeup: Deevetkeo Grisseth
Stylist: Rodney High

Printed in the United States of America

Be-You-Tiful
Jada Collins

1. Title 2. Author 3. Self-Help

LCCN: 2007903048

ISBN 10: 0-9795856-0-0
ISBN 13: 978-0-9795856-0-9

In Memory of

John H. Johnson

1918–2005

*My deepest condolences to Eunice W. Johnson, Linda Johnson Rice, Alexa Rice
and the entire Johnson family. I will never forget what John has done for me.
The legacy he leaves behind will continue to inspire millions around the world.*

DEDICATION

With heart-felt sentiments,
I would like to dedicate this book to...

My wonderful husband, Ernest Collins, Jr., who taught me the
importance of loving life and loving myself.

My amazing mother, Barbara Hines Jackson (BJ),
who encouraged me to forgive and forget.

My father, Isaac Jackson, who educated me on life's toughest lessons,
but most of all, who showed me that through God's
amazing grace, we are covered by the blood of the Lamb.
Old things are passed away and all things are renewed.

My beautiful sister, Charise Jackson, who demonstrates, through
example, the importance of loving—no matter what.

My Aunt Dolores, who always believed in me.

My grandmother, Eugenia Jackson, as well as my family and friends,
who loved me when I didn't, or couldn't, love myself.

To my wonderful friends, who have been there when I needed them
most. I don't want to forget you: Rebecca Beasley, Angela (Tee) Brown,
Staci R. Collins, Theresa Davis, Jacqueline Gill, Michelle Gill,
Tinika Blackmon, Dereka Hendon, Rodney High,
Princess Monique, Bruce Petrie and Steve Williams.
Of course, there are others, but too many to name.

And last but not least, my extraordinary godmother, Claudette Hamilton,
who dedicated her life to teaching me everything that I know.

ACKNOWLEDGEMENTS

To Terri Liggins Stingley, who helped me write and edit this book…Thank you for your tireless hours and unselfish spirit from start to finish. You are a wonderful woman of God!

To Erica Crawford, an awesome graphic designer… Thank you for your immeasurable time and effort in pulling this project together. Your creativity is truly amazing!

To Staci R. Collins, thank you for additional editing and coaching… You are a brilliant young woman!

Again, to my wonderful Husband for EVERYTHING: additional editing, proofreading, coaching, writing, brainstorming and pampering! Thanks for being there when I needed you the most!

And a most gracious thank you to my friends, family and colleagues whose contributions through proofreading, critiquing or in any other way, helped to bring my story alive.

I appreciate you all. God bless!

Love,
Jada

BE-You-TIFUL

THEORY

There are three elements of our being that make up our existence. Vast and unique, this human "trinity" is composed of the body, soul and spirit, which reflect the image and wisdom of God.

As we move through the chapters of this book, I hope my testimony demonstrates the process by which all three parts work together toward becoming "you." I'd like to be transparent in revealing struggles I've dealt with in life, to show readers that trials and tribulations don't define us and that through God's guidance, our troubles are used to refine us. Although the process can seem overwhelming, the outcome always manifests something that's Be-You-Tiful.

Be You

Be: To be or to exist without force or strain, to have presence with consistency and without effort.

You: An individual's character, personality, feelings, touch, tastes, voice, talents and gifts.

Tiful (full): Holding as much as is possible. Nothing missing or lacking. To be full of God's spirit.

TABLE OF CONTENTS

PROLOGUE

HER PIERCING SCREAMS gripped me in the darkness of night, giving voice to the terror I had seen in her eyes so many times. My heart stampeded in my breast; blood thundered in my ears. I could sense her fear, but I could not even begin to imagine her pain. Why was this happening? I wanted to scream, too—just to drown out her cries of despair. Blood ran cold through my body, in dissonant harmony with the hot tears that streamed down my cheeks. Fear paralyzed me.

The night was filled with blackness and despair. No way out. I saw only darkness. I heard only screams of terror and rage. I tasted only the salt of my tears.

I huddled against the headboard of my bed, praying that he would not come after me, or my little sister, who was on the bottom bunk. I knew she was afraid of him, too, but neither of us spoke a word—we just lay there in silence and prayed.

"Say something now, b****!" my father yelled. "Say something *now!*"

I desperately wanted to help my mother. I wished I could help her. I wished I could make him stop. But I couldn't. My mother's screams grew more intense as the shatter and crash of breaking glass filled our small, two-bedroom house.

My sister began to cry. I jumped down from the top bunk and climbed into bed with her. I was eight years old; she was six. It was my job to protect her. I lived to protect her—not just because it came naturally, but because she *trusted* me.

Now, she grabbed me and held on, as if to keep from falling. "I want my mommy," she cried.

That night, my father beat my mother with a broom. My sister and I had grown accustomed to the abuse by then, but that particular night, his rage crescendoed to an unbearable level. I thought he truly hated us.

Soon, the yelling stopped and I heard a sound that called a sigh of relief from my very soul. Who would have thought that the harsh sound of a slamming door could bring comfort? But it did. He was gone. It was over...for now.

I never understood why my mother wasn't good enough for Dad. As valedictorian of her high school class, she had proven her intelligence. Her curvaceous body had always turned men's heads, but she was too modest to notice—at least, I thought it was modesty, but I now recognize it as lack of self-esteem. I thought she was beautiful, but her beauty wasn't good enough for my father. Not only did he abuse her, but he cheated on her. The slamming door probably heralded a visit to one of his many girlfriends.

That night ended with me drifting off to sleep with my younger sister holding on to me for dear life. The next day greeted us with a false sense of normalcy; my mother woke us and rushed us to get ready for school, just as she did every day, as if nothing had happened. I cried all that morning. I got a spanking from my mother because I didn't know—and couldn't explain—*why* I was crying.

I suppose I cried because I hated life, but the spanking didn't help me to know that any better.

⚜

My father once said to me, "You're just like your ugly momma."

Things that people say to us as kids stick. We don't realize it when we're small, but those words are playing over and over in the back of our minds like a broken record. Back then I didn't realize it, but with those six simple words, my father disabled me. Those six words would rise up to haunt me in so many situations in my life, ruining my enjoyment, sabotaging my relationships.

But at the same time, that cruel collection of words set my course in life in ways I can only look back on in wonder.

As I grew older, I developed an intolerable bitterness and resentment toward my father and toward all men. But even more than I hated men, I was terrified of them. Nor did I understand them—not a bit. Their inexplicable behavior raised a host of unanswerable questions in my head: *What was wrong with being like my mother? Why did my father call such a beautiful woman ugly? Why did he yell and curse at her? Why did he beat her? And if I was like my mother, would I be treated that way as well?*

I daydreamed my way through my early years, hoping I would be rescued from the torture of having been born. By the time I was ten, I wanted to die or run away. Until I thought about my little sister. I had to stick around for her sake. She was the only one who really needed me; the only one who really loved me. I couldn't let her down. So, I stayed right there and lived for *her.*

Words are powerful things. I talked about how my father's words disabled me. The year our family moved to Rodeo, California, a small town just twenty miles north of San Francisco, I experienced the other side of words.

We'd relocated to be closer to my maternal grandmother, Ann Lee, who also lived in Rodeo. We welcomed a new school, new friends, a fresh start.

One day during lunch, one of my classmates kidded with me about a boy named Greg, who presumably had a crush on me. *Me?* I couldn't believe it. *Someone actually had a crush on me?* My heart fluttered with joy. *Wow, someone likes me.*

My friend Gina said, "Yeah, I knew that. He thinks you're pretty—like a model."

Pretty like a model. These words were different; the tone was different. They were words of acceptance, and I liked hearing them. They reconnected me with life. The tone was positive, approving...and refreshing to hear. *Me, a model?* I thought with utter disbelief. Suddenly, I felt like a million dollars.

Such is the power of words. It took six to disable me—only four to enable me. From that day on, I held fast to the hope that my father was wrong. Maybe I wasn't ugly after all. Someone actually thought I was pretty. Someone actually thought that I could become a model. It didn't matter that the opinion was that of a goofy-acting, spitball-throwing, fifth grade boy. It was a major boost for my confidence. I went from being strung out on negativity to being addicted to that precious thing called hope.

Today, as I reflect on my journey, one thing comes to mind: If I had known then what I know now, if I had been able to see the way my life would turn out, I could have avoided so much misery. I would have known that those words-those two sentences spoken by a man and a boy-had each, in its own way, set my destiny in motion.

So, here is the Question now burning in my soul: How many young girls and women are experiencing the same pain I endured with no knowledge, hope or help to overcome it?

The Question has led me to a Goal: to share my life's story. And the Purpose of that Goal is to build hope through encouragement, and to impart knowledge through testimony, so that some other young girl or woman may be inspired to overcome her circumstances and find the courage and self-confidence to live in accordance with God's plan for her life.

I don't profess to have all the answers, but what I will confess to you is my faith in Jesus Christ. He is the reason for me overcoming all my fears. I have learned one valuable lesson in life, that everything starts and ends with God. The Bible tells us that Jesus is the Author and Perfecter of our faith (Hebrews 12:2) and that everything that happens to us—everything that's *said* to us—has a reason. It only works toward bringing out our hidden beauty and our glorious potential.

So my question to you is: Who do you think has the final word about what we go through in life?

I've listened to the words of my Dad, my Momma, my friends—everyone else. Their words were sometimes so loud in my ears, I couldn't hear God's word. In his letter to the Roman congregation, the Apostle Paul wrote: "Faith comes by hearing the message, and the message is heard through the word of Christ." (Romans 10:17)

Hearing and *understanding* is the key to believing anything. All it took for me to believe negative, hurtful things about myself was *hearing* them spoken over and over again. So you can imagine how important it was for me to hear the truth about me, so I could *become* me.

Who are you listening to? Where are you getting your information about yourself? Let's face it, when it comes to your life, *there are only two opinions that really matter:* yours and God's. God says that you are beautifully and wonderfully made. What do *you* say?

We are all works-in-progress, and every test can be turned into a testimony. Every testimony can inspire healing and, yes, sometimes healing can start with the simple revelation that you are beautiful!

CHAPTER ONE

Nowhere to Hide

LIFE IS A STAGE. At least, that's what William Shakespeare said. On the stage of my life, there've been good guys, bad guys and everything in between. Every actor has his own role to play, his own lines, his own stage business. Sometimes he says his lines and does his business without thinking about how it's going to affect the other characters. Most of our lives are like that, I suspect. A mixed bag. But let me take a moment to set the stage for *my* life—introduce the cast of characters. The curtain's open; the spotlight is bright; there's nowhere to hide.

The Cast—My Dysfunctional Family

My Father: Isaac Jackson is a tall, strikingly handsome man of six feet, four inches, with a butterscotch complexion and light-brown eyes. I definitely got my height from his side of the family. My father had lots of friends; everyone seemed to like him. Everyone, that is, except me, my mother, and sister—we were afraid of him.

My Mother: At only five feet, four inches, Barbara Jackson—we called her BJ—stood a whole foot shorter than her husband. Her beautiful skin and dainty, curvaceous body made her the object of men's catcalls. She didn't notice—she couldn't imagine they were whistling at her.

My Baby Sister: Rece, which is short for Charise Jackson, is two years my junior. She always looked to me for security and love–two very important things I never received, but somehow always knew how to give to her. It was my job to protect her—because I loved her, and because all we had was each other. We were close. Fear drew us even closer.

Me: Chanese Marie Jackson, (the name change came later) abused and full of hatred towards a lot of things. As much as I loved my mother because she *was* my mother, I also disliked her. I longed for her to nurture me in a way she just couldn't seem to do. My father made it almost impossible to love him, so disliking and fearing him was easy.

❧

My parents were both abusive and neglectful, but I learned something important from them. I learned that messing up your life is a fulltime job; it keeps you too busy to be concerned about much else—even the people who love you.

My mother worked so many hours that I rarely saw her. She left her little girls with a variety of caregivers, allowing them to mold and shape our lives. When we were lucky enough to spend time with her, it wasn't quality time; it was time at her job while she was working.

Time with my father? Now there's a joke. As a probation officer at juvenile hall, he made decent money. But he worked long hours to do it. In case there's any doubt, let me tell you: in a child's eyes, money is no substitute for time and attention.

My father's absence left my mother as the lone caregiver for my sister and me. In that role, she was bitter and sweet—a real Dr. Jekyll and Mr. Hyde personality. Deep down I suppose I knew she loved us—after all, she worked hard to support us. But I saw everything she did through the dark lenses of abuse and neglect. Life had written her a part she didn't know how to play, so she improvised.

It boggles my mind to think of how many other women are trapped in similar roles, unable to find the exit. It seems simple and logical (at least for those on the outside looking in) for a woman to leave an abusive husband. But in reality, it's the hardest and most difficult decision for an abused woman to make.

It also seems logical to think that, if a young girl grows up seeing abuse, she'll do anything to avoid it in her own relationships. Yet later in life, I found myself in the very same muddle. And I can tell you that walking away from that torture was, emotionally, the hardest thing I've ever had to do. Why? Because for me—and millions of others—abuse got all mixed up with love. Abuse is like a snare. When love gets tangled up in it, it sucks all the sanctity and sincerity out of it.

I think we must be taught love—what it is, how it looks, feels, sounds. If we have no one to teach us that, we can't tell real love from all the other things that masquerade as love: lust, dependency, need, fear of being alone.

Love is an attribute of God. The Apostle Paul says that: "Love is patient and kind; love does not envy or boast; it is not arrogant or rude. It does not insist on its own way; it is not irritable or resentful; it does not rejoice at wrongdoing, but rejoices with the truth. Love bears all things, believes all things, hopes all things, endures all things." (1 Corinthians 13:4-7)

Love bears all things, even abuse. This is why it is vital to know *real* love—to know its sound, its touch, its taste, its behavior—and to love wisely. Because it is oh-so-difficult to set love aside.

ꙮ

By age ten, I'd already been exposed to inappropriate behavior with boys. Some of this inappropriate "touching" occurred while I was visiting my maternal grandmother, Ann Lee, and involved a variety of male members of our extended family and friends.

How did I feel about that? I felt guilty. I felt afraid. I felt confused. I *hated* the way I felt.

One Fourth of July, our relatives gathered at my aunt's house. All the parents were there with their kids—except my father. My father never came. He was never around; but Lord knows I needed him around then. An older boy—a so-called friend of the family—led me into a bedroom at the back of the house. When we got there, he began to pull down my pants.

"What are you doing?" I shrieked in fear.

"Just watch, I'm going to show you something," he said, as if we were playing a game.

I was only ten, but I knew the games he wanted to play were meant only for adults. I still trusted him because he was a "friend," and because I mistook his attention for love.

Imagine that—fearful and trusting all at the same time. As we stood face to face, he pulled down his pants, and then pulled down mine. He proceeded to press his bare, erect penis against my naked pelvic bone, moving his body from side to side against mine, as though we were slow dancing. He pressed harder. He moved faster.

"Wait," I said, my heart galloping, "Someone's coming!" And I wasn't kidding—someone really was moving down the hall toward the bedroom.

Determined to not have his game interrupted, he quickly shoved me into the closet and closed the door. I wasn't sure I liked this game. It didn't hurt, but it just seemed *wrong*.

Strangely, I thought about my father every time I found myself in a situation like this. *What would Daddy say?* My daddy could protect me from anything and everything if he wanted to, I told myself. For some reason, he just didn't want to.

I was scared. Scared of what would happen if we were caught lying in the bottom of a dark closet with our pants down. The sounds of footsteps passed. He wanted to continue playing his game. All I wanted was my daddy. But we did what *he* wanted.

The closet was just large enough for me to lie on top of some shoes and for him to lie on top of me. With my eyes shut tight, I grimaced in pain— partly due to my frenzied shame, and partly due to the shoes poking my back. The boy was deep in concentration, oblivious to anything I might have felt. He just kept on with his game, pressing and rubbing against me.

Suddenly, he stiffened, letting out a strange, strangled grunt. I peeked at him to see what he would do next. He simply got up, opened the closet door, zipped up his pants and walked out of the room.

"Where are you going?" I whispered as I scrambled up and pulled on my own pants.

He didn't hear me; he didn't even *try* to hear me. He was gone.

What just happened? What did I do? Confused, I left the room to find my mother. She was sitting on a sofa in the family room, talking to the other grownups. I slid next to her and did not move until it was time to go home.

✿

On the surface, we seemed like a normal family, I suppose: a tall, handsome father; a beautiful, loving wife; and two healthy, obedient little girls. We lived in Rodeo, California: middle-class suburbia. Your typical, Eighties style of comfortable living.

But our beautiful, four-bedroom home provided the perfect front for a severely dysfunctional family. My mother, sister and I went to church every Sunday without Dad. He rarely went anywhere with us, and we never went anywhere with him. Our family wasn't big on talking, either. In fact I don't recall that we ever sat down to talk about anything. We did not eat dinner together. We didn't do anything together. We were strangers co-existing behind closed doors, merely looking normal. Inside, we were broken.

There was one bright spot: my sister and I visited our paternal grandparents almost every weekend. They lived in Richmond, California, just ten miles south of Rodeo. My grandmother had a beautiful collection of teddy bears. I suppose that explains why, to this day, stuffed animals make me smile. There is something wonderfully innocent about a stuffed animal.

On my birthday, my grandparents gave me cool gifts or money—usually in the amount of one-hundred dollars. I preferred gifts to money because when I got money, my parents would take it, and I'd never see it again.

If I could have asked for any gift in the world, I would have asked for unambiguous love. I can say that now; but at the age of ten, what little girl thinks to ask for love as a gift? It's a parent's duty to give it. But my father didn't love me because I reminded him of my mother. My mother didn't love me because she didn't know how. And I hadn't a clue about how to change that.

❧

Ann Lee didn't love me either. We called her that: Ann Lee. We never called her Grandma. Every Sunday after church we went over to her house. I didn't like church. I liked going to Ann Lee's even less.

"Close the damn door before you let flies in the house!" was our usual greeting as we walked in from church. She had a way about her, Ann Lee did—a way of threatening us into obedience. "Sit yo' black butts down before I beat you with my hammer!"

And if it wasn't the *hammer*, then it was the *broom*. I didn't want to be hit by either of them, so I obeyed. It wasn't until I was about thirteen that I realized she only meant to scare us with that hammer, she'd never actually beat us.

Ann Lee had been born with a degenerative spinal disease, which left her right arm totally paralyzed and her other limbs next to useless. She walked with a rolling limp and required constant care. As the oldest girl in our extended family, a great deal of that responsibility fell to me. At Ann Lee's house, it was my duty to ensure that everything got done. At age ten, I washed and cleaned better than some adults. I paid my grandmother's bills, grocery shopped and dressed her.

In return, Ann Lee embarrassed us. She especially seemed to enjoy cussing us out in front of our friends—a sure means of total humiliation. If I ever happened to have a friend with me at Ann Lee's house, there was a great chance my grandmother would give her something to tease me about at school the next day...before an audience. Cruelty is something some people feel compelled to pass along.

One hot summer day, my mother dropped Rece and I off at Ann Lee's one-bedroom, project apartment. I felt abandoned, unloved and unwanted. What else was new? We had grown accustomed to being dropped off there; but on this particular day, I could feel my blood boiling. I knew Ann Lee didn't want us there any more than we wanted to be there. She was doing her daughter a favor by babysitting us; I was doing her a favor by taking care of her. You'd think those two things would cancel each other out and we'd be even, but somehow Ann Lee seemed to imagine that we owed her.

I can't recall what sparked it, but Ann Lee started yelling at me. I wanted to leave so badly I could taste it, but I had nowhere to go. So I stood at the front door looking out through the screen. My cousins and their friends sat on the front porch, laughing at my humiliation. My heart pounded with embarrassment, anxiety, and resentment—all rolled into one huge ache.

I wish she would shut up! I want to go home. I want to get away, I thought. My back to my grandmother, who sat at the table across the room, I hid that great big ache as best as I could. I thought I was doing a great job of it, too, until the tears began streaming down my cheeks.

Before I knew what happened, anger rose up out of my heart, knotted itself in my throat, and spewed out through my mouth. With as much force as I could muster, I spun to face my grandmother and screamed, "Shut up, you crippled old b****!" Hate's venom dripped from every word.

My blood ran cold. Silence swallowed up all sound in the room. I can't remember who else was in the apartment, but all talking and activity just *stopped.* The only sound came from a small television on the table that played a rerun of *Good Times.* I turned my back on Ann Lee and continued to stare out through the screen. I tried to ignore the open mouths of my cousins and their friends. A moment later, I heard my grandmother's halting steps shuffling away from me down the hall.

An earthquake of guilt shook me, and my heart melted with compassion. Had I just called my grandmother a *cripple*? And the *b-word*? Yes, I had done those things—said those things. Disrespecting my grandmother (no matter how cruel a despot she was) was wrong. I had to apologize. After a few deep breaths to muster up some courage, I went back to her bedroom.

Ann Lee had her back to the door and stood peering out her window. Startled by my sudden appearance, she backed up to her bed and plopped down on it, wiping tears from her eyes. She was *crying*.

Sobbing, I gave her a hug and apologized. She cried even harder.

For the first time in my life, I realized that my grandmother had feelings. She'd never showed that side before. Only the side that called me a "little hussy" showed. Only the side that threatened me with the hammer and the broom showed. Only the side that cursed like a sailor and had more talk than Muhammad Ali showed.

But in that brief moment, holding her and crying with her, the reality struck me that my grandmother hurt just as I did.

Ann Lee is gone now. If I could go back in time and undo some things, I would. I harbored a lot of bitterness and anger toward her. It hurts me now to think about how difficult her life must have been. And she could no more run away from her life than I could.

I can now look back at that unpleasant situation and see how the anger and bitterness I experienced in my home affected me in other environments. My Dad was so mean to me that, in turn, I found myself being mean to others. Negativity breeds negativity. Since then, I've learned that we are responsible for our own actions and reactions.

꧁꧂

At an early age, I learned to "hold my tongue" in front of Daddy—not because I didn't have an opinion, but because I feared getting beaten to a pulp for saying what I felt. It was ironic, really—I was at once fearful and fearless. I was terrified of my father, but I'd challenge Sugar Ray Leonard to a fistfight, believing that I could win. That's because what Daddy lacked in parental love and support, he made up for with lessons on how to fight.

"Never come home a loser," he'd tell me. And when he wanted to make a strong point, he usually started his sentence with, "Don't come home if…" For example: "Don't come home if you lose a fight." "Don't come home if you're with a white boy." Funny, though, I never heard: "Don't come home if you have a bad report card." "Don't come home if you do something bad in school."

He didn't seem to care if I got an "A" or an "F."

❧

The pastor of our church once said that the mind holds onto negative things, and the positive things are what we have to force it to remember. That certainly explains why some terrible images of my childhood replay vividly in my mind as though they happened just yesterday.

Take the night we were coming back from a rare outing at a drive-in movie. It must have been around two in the morning. My sister and I were fast asleep in the back seat, and were awakened by my mother's terrified screams and my father's loud cursing.

"Get out of the car!" Dad roared.

My heart started to pound. My mind curled into protective mode as I pulled my little sister under my arm. *Please don't get out of the car; don't leave us alone with him,* I begged Momma silently. But then again, the best thing for her would have been to get out of that car and walk away.

"You ain't nothin'!" he yelled as he steered with his left hand and slapped my mother with his right. He yelled profanities at her. Then with one harsh, open-handed shove, he slammed her head against the window with a disturbing thud.

I decided right then and there that I would kill my father—someday, somehow. My paternal grandma owned a gun. I would work out a plan to steal that gun and kill him.

It sounds horrible, doesn't it? An eleven-year-old girl contemplating killing her own Daddy? But that was the depth of my desperation—I wanted nothing but to stop him from hurting us anymore. And the only way I could think of to do that was to make him go away—for good.

Then again, I couldn't kill him. How would we live without him? What if someone broke into our house? I knew that my dad would protect us if anyone tried to hurt us. As far as I was concerned, my father could take on anybody. He certainly could kick my mother's behind.

That was my childhood in a nutshell: I hated my father and wanted to kill him. I loved my father and desperately wanted his protection and approval. I was terrified at the prospect of life without him.

One weekend, my mother took Rece and me on a church trip to Disneyland. We were gone for two days. When we returned, our house had been stripped of almost everything. Panicking, my momma dashed from room to room, thinking we had been robbed. But we hadn't been robbed; my father had simply left us. Without warning.

My mother stood in an empty living room crying like a baby. Rece and I cried with her, in a moment of shared grief. He'd abandoned us. And he had taken everything that I had known to be a part of my life. The sofa, the coffee table, the pictures…everything. How could he be so cruel?

And who would protect us now?

That was the last straw. I thought I was going to have a nervous breakdown for sure. That night, my mother dropped us off at Ann Lee's house and disappeared for several months. During that time, my sister and I had no mother. No father. All we had was each other.

My life completely changed in that one night. Not only did my father leave us, but my mother abandoned us as well. I didn't know it at the time, but I found out later that my father had threatened to kill Momma and my aunts were literally *hiding* her. On top of everything else, she was having a mental breakdown. Can you blame her?

To say I had mixed emotions about my father abandoning us is to understate the situation. I couldn't believe he'd leave us emotionally, psychologically, and mentally violated like that. On the other hand, I wanted Momma to be safe, so maybe it was better for her that he was gone. But she'd dumped me in an environment where I'd find myself constantly looking over my shoulder, hoping that I wouldn't continue to be sexually molested by the so-called friends and relatives who frequented my grandmother's home. I had nowhere to run and nowhere to hide.

By the time I reached the sixth grade, I was a complete basket case, but something kept me hanging on by a thread. Seventh grade found me desperately in search of a way out. A refuge.

That summer, I found it.

BE-You-TIFUL
TRINITY

Be You
PRACTICAL APPLICATION

In unpleasant situations, many of us find ourselves backed against the wall with nowhere to hide. In these situations I've learned that two things are of critical importance:

1. That I understand my purpose.
2. That I attempt to replace the negative in my life with the positive.

In my quest to become "me," I have adopted a few concepts and Godly principals that have encouraged me along the way. I believe they can help you, too. Here's my Be-You-Tiful "Trinity."

1) **Replace the negative with the positive**
As a child, I was in search of a refuge. I didn't know it then, but I would later discover that submerging myself in various activities could relieve me of much pain. Although this may not seem like a spiritual solution, we can't take for granted the simple positive things that God may put in our lives to help us through hurt and pain.
So until you *overcome* what you're going through, do yourself a favor and continue living your life *by engaging in your purpose*. For me, at the age of eleven, that was cheerleading. Today, it is modeling, being a public speaker and an author.
What is your positive passion? Find it and use it as your refuge. Learn to replace life's negativity with positive thought, action and worship.

2) Recognize that pain is inevitable.

Prepare yourself for life's disappointments and frustrations. *Expect* obstacles and difficulties. We can never completely eliminate all risks, but with the understanding that they are coming, we can plan accordingly. When we understand this law of life, we can begin to let the healing process take place.

It was a challenge for me to recognize that the unpleasant things I had to face were just part of life. *Everyone* faces them. I had to be honest with myself about this in order to have the healing process run its full course. This meant I had to stop blaming other people for whatever happened to me.

Consider this: If another person's name comes up every time you discuss your pain, then you haven't accepted *your* responsibility in the healing process.

I'm not saying that it's okay for one person to abuse, molest or hurt another, but I had to learn that *what's done is done* and that I was in charge of my life and how I reacted to the abuse. If I buckled to it, let it make me bitter, then the abusers in my life won, and I surely didn't want that!

Remember this: *God may use pain to teach us, but it becomes our responsibility to learn from it and better ourselves. Sometimes pain will teach you what pride won't let you learn.*

3) Don't be afraid to face your pain.

The biggest problems we face today often are not our afflictions, but *our pride in dealing with those afflictions.* We're too proud to admit weakness, to acknowledge that we've been hurt. But healing from any form of abuse or hurt will only begin at the point we *expose* that hurt. So don't try to hide your pain. Mental and emotional pain is just like a physical condition, the longer you put off going to see a doctor, the worse it may get.

Remember: *What you fail to confront today will be there waiting for you to face tomorrow.*

CHAPTER TWO

Searching

REFUGE, FOR ME, CAME IN THE FORM OF cheerleading, of all things. I tried out for a community cheerleading squad, earned my position, paid the entry fee and became a cheerleader! This became my long sought after get-away. We practiced all summer long. With my mother at work all the time and my father nowhere to be found, no one cared where I was. Many days I wandered around the streets of Rodeo—where we now lived with Ann Lee—anxiously anticipating each cheerleading practice.

For the first time in my life, I felt a sense of belonging. I enjoyed being needed. Those girls needed me to complete the formations, to complete the team. My inner spirit had finally awakened in the midst of a bunch of giggling girls, who prided themselves in jumping up and down, screaming chants and waving their arms all over the place. Sounds like a synopsis for a grade B movie: Girl finds self-worth in a cheerleading squad!

As the first game approached, I called my father to invite him. The other girls' mothers and fathers were coming, so I took a chance. What was I thinking? I called his number repeatedly, leaving message after message. He never called back; never acknowledged my call; never acknowledged my existence. Because he never called back, I disliked him even more. How dare he ignore his own flesh and blood? I settled in my mind that my father was Satan himself—void of any compassion for anyone, perhaps not even himself.

After my father left, we never heard much from him. One day, I called his mother and he just happened to be at her house. We spoke, but the conversation was superficial. He hesitantly gave me his new home phone number.

Now why, you might ask, should I care whether or not that no-good, two-timing, sorry-excuse-for-a-father wanted to give his phone number to his own daughter? Well, for starters, I cared because I still wanted him to love me. I wanted to be "daddy's little girl." I wanted him to hold me, protect me and be there when I needed him. And I needed him every day of my life, though he was nowhere to be found.

Well, neither of my parents showed up for that first game, or any other. So I cheered for myself and for Rece, ignoring that pair of empty seats. Rece became a cheerleader, too, making the squad for her age group. She and I caught the bus to and from all the games, supporting each other in cheerleading as in all things.

Rece didn't handle our parents' break-up well. She often cried herself to sleep and had bad dreams. She cried for loneliness and I cried for her because her pain was so deep. She was sick a lot as a child, too, suffering often from diarrhea and vomiting.

"I want my daddy," she'd tell me. She loved our father—certainly more than I did—but then, she was too young to fully understand some things about him, so her love hadn't been as thoroughly crushed as mine had. All she knew was that she missed him.

I knew I hated him.

⁂

Our cheerleading squad worked tirelessly all summer long on a routine for a statewide competition. We won first place. That was the best feeling ever! I couldn't remember being so excited—so charged—about anything in my entire life. I had found my niche—something that I was good at and that came naturally to me. Dancing also came naturally to me. I felt better about myself when I danced. I welcomed this sense of accomplishment and self-worth as it was long overdue.

Cheerleading also brought me a new circle of girlfriends. These friends usually had two things on their minds: boyfriends and sex. Well, maybe that's one thing. They cared intensely about who'd gotten a boyfriend, who'd lost a boyfriend and who'd lost her virginity. Each time these topics came up, I shuddered at the thought of someone finding out about my embarrassing and disgusting encounters with the opposite sex. I prayed no one would. I actually thought I had had sex already, not knowing what "sex" really was. My mother never talked to my sister and I about those kinds of things. I didn't even know anything about my menstrual cycle until I got my first period.

I didn't understand why my mother cared so little about us, why she left us with Ann Lee so much, why she allowed us to just wander through life. How can you have children and be totally negligent of their needs, their wants and especially their pain? Whether they want to be or not, parents are the road map to success or failure for their children. I needed my mother to love me and point me in the right direction. I guess she just didn't know how.

As a young child, I could remember at times clinging to my mother's leg or hip, and she would tell me to go and sit down. It hurt to have her push me away. I wanted her to tell me that she loved me. I wanted her to tell me that I was beautiful…that my sister was beautiful…that she, herself, was beautiful…that we were *all* beautiful and that Daddy didn't know what he was talking about. We were not ugly. We were beautiful black women. But she never said any of those things, so I continued to think my father *did* know what he was talking about when he said I was ugly.

Growing up in predominantly white schools only intensified my insecurities. As one of the only black girls in my class, I stood out. Looking back, I now realize that could have been an advantage for me; however, at the time, it spelled more heartache. Not only was I ugly by my father's standards, but an alien by my schoolmates' standards. I was tall for an eleven-year-old girl. I had long, skinny legs—not model's legs but Olive Oyl's legs. Kids called me that—Olive Oyl. They also came up with Giraffe, Beanpole and Tree. I learned to not let the name-calling bother me. I developed a tough skin—it hurt, but I could take it.

In the sixth grade, our school did a production of *Grease*. I loved the movie, and I loved to dance; so I signed up to audition for a role as one of twenty dancers. It came as no surprise that I was the lone black girl trying out for this play. We auditioned with "The Car Dance" (the scene performed by John Travolta and his gang in the movie). I bubbled with uncontrollable excitement on the day of auditions and, putting my whole heart into it, I won a part. Our costumes were blue jeans, white t-shirts and black shoes— all things I would have to borrow, as money was tight.

After a week of rehearsals, we dancers asked if we could entertain the lunch crowd in the cafeteria. We were excited for the opportunity to per-form in front of our peers. After school, I practiced and practiced. I told everyone that I would be dancing at lunchtime the next day. I borrowed a white t-shirt from one of my cousins and a pair of jeans from a friend. I didn't have black shoes, so I wore white sneakers (and to my relief, when I arrived at school the next day, many of the other dancers wore white sneak-ers as well). We rehearsed between classes in preparation for our lunchtime debut. Right before the performance, one of the lead dancers took me aside to have a word with me.

"I watched *Grease* last night," she began archly, "and I don't think you should be in the dance because there were no black people in the movie, and we want our dance to be like the movie." Having blurted that out, she nodded at the other dancers, encouraging their agreement with her. Then, mission accomplished, and with a flip of her short brown hair, the girl left.

I couldn't believe I'd heard her right. She hadn't said that, hadn't *meant* that. I'd *earned* that part! I deserved to be in that play like everyone else—regardless of my color! My heart drummed in my ears and felt as if it wanted to leap out of my chest. Perspiration beaded up all over me. I was so angry, I wanted to hit her; yet somehow humiliation outweighed the anger, so I cried instead. They were tears of disbelief. Being singled out for taunting—because of my looks or my color—wasn't new, but this time the thick skin I thought I'd developed had proved paper-thin.

I was the best dancer, I shouted after her mentally. How could they get rid of me because of my color?

Well, much to her disappointment, they couldn't. The others refused to side with her; in fact, some argued in my defense. They knew I was the best dancer.

She grudgingly agreed to me staying in the dance, but assigned me to the back row. I danced, but hardly anyone saw me.

※

I often found myself faced with prejudice. So much that I decided I wanted to be white. I *hated* being black. From the day I came to that deci-sion, things changed. I changed. Life changed. My goals changed. Before I'd wanted to stand out. Now, I just wanted to fit in. I wanted to be like them—the white girls. I wanted to dress like them, but I didn't have enough money. I wanted to go where they went, but my parents were never around to take me anywhere. But in all that wanting, I realized that no matter how I dressed, talked or acted, my skin color would never change.

Anthony, a black classmate, helped me to realize that even more. Anthony was the first boy I ever had a crush on. It started in the fourth grade and continued way too long, until about the ninth grade. He never gave me the time of day. He never even looked my way. In fact, one day when he *did* look my way, he actually told me I didn't stand a chance with him because I didn't have blonde hair and blue eyes. Now I really felt like the ugliest girl in the school…and as confused as ever.

In all that confusion, I still found time to sit and daydream about how successful I would be someday. To be honest, there were days I didn't care what anyone thought of me. I didn't care if they thought I was ugly. I didn't care if they were mean to me because of my skin color.

In my mind, I excelled at everything. As a result, I persisted. As a result, I developed a truly tough skin. As a result, I maintained my sanity because even at the young age of twelve, I could have easily gone out of my mind.

BE-You-TIFUL
TRINITY

Perfect Fit
PRACTICAL APPLICATION

The question to which I found myself constantly in search of an answer was: *Where do I fit?* I didn't feel significant at home. I didn't fit in at school. I felt like an outsider at church.

Have you ever worn a pair of shoes that didn't quite fit? Did you notice that, after a while, you began walking differently to compensate for the discomfort?

There's an important lesson in this: Just because that metaphorical pair of shoes *looks* right doesn't mean they *are* right. You've got to make sure that they fit and *feel* right so they don't bring harm to you.

As a model, I look for the perfect fit in my clothes, as do most people. If something does not fit right, either I won't wear it, or I'll take steps to improve the garment so that it feels and looks right on *me*. I use the same principle in my everyday life. Instead of trying desperately to *fit*, I try to remember all the things I possess that fit me perfectly.

Keep this in mind when you're attempting to find what fits and doesn't fit in life. If you have to squeeze or force your way into situations or relationships, then they're probably not good fits.

Take the "Fit" Test

There are three things that happen when you're trying too hard to fit into something:

1. Loss of Confidence
2. Comparison and Competition
3. Pain and Disappointment

Here's a set of three questions about "fit" that apply to that human trinity of body, mind and spirit:

1) **What is your *physical* body type?** I mean this literally, not metaphorically. Are you attempting to squeeze into a size eight when you are clearly a size twelve? Do you make decisions about your wardrobe with preconceived notions of what someone will say or think of you? Like everyone else, you are created in the image and likeness of God, and yet remain unique among human beings. There is no one who compares with you. The Apostle Paul even speaks of this: "Each one should test his own actions. Then he can take pride in himself, without comparing himself to somebody else…" (Galatians 6:4) *Be careful not to fall into* **comparison and competition** *with others.*

2) **What is your *mental* "shoe size"—your capacity?** Be careful of trying to fit into someone else's shoes: your boss', your favorite movie star's, a supermodel's or even those of a friend you admire. Don't waste valuable time thinking about how to wear the same style and size as those you may envy or hold in high esteem. Instead, take the time to perfect your own gifts so that you *don't* **lose confidence** *in the talents and abilities that God gave you.*

3) **What is your *spiritual* fitness level?** Are you fit and ready to handle the pressure of being rejected by the "in" crowd? Rejection may make us feel we've lost the love and acceptance of others, but we can't make the mistake of seeking validation by forcing ourselves to fit in. Accepting guidance from and "working out" with the Holy Spirit is the only way to stay in spiritual shape. *Don't let the* **pain** *and* **disappointments** *in life sap your strength.*

We try a lot of things on for size, but it's only when we're clothed in our right minds and hearts that we are ready for true success.

CHAPTER THREE

Who, Me?

A BRIGHT GLEAM OF HOPE came in the form of my aunt Rachel, my mother's youngest sister. I idolized Rachel. At twenty-five, she was old enough to be cool, yet young enough to understand me. I could understand her. She enjoyed listening to me; that meant she cared. I loved her just for caring about me.

Aunt Rachel served in the Army. I loved hearing her stories, even though her experiences terrified me. One thing I knew I would never do was join the Army. During her leaves-of-absence, she taught me a lot: how to care for my hair and nails, what boys were all about and how to drive a stick-shift car. I learned all those things in the seventh grade.

One piece of advice she instilled in me was, "Don't take no crap from nobody; *especially* a man." At twelve, I didn't quite understand what she meant by that, but I certainly do now. "Don't take no crap," she would chant, laughing and waving her finger. That became our motto.

It was my aunt Rachel who first inspired me to pursue modeling. "How tall are you?" she asked one day, looking me up and down from her seat on Ann Lee's tattered sofa, which doubled as a bed for Rece and me.

"I'm five-nine," I said with certainty. I knew that because I tracked my growth with a watchful eye, desperately hoping that it would *stop*. I hated being tall. At the time, I couldn't imagine that I would grow another two inches before graduating from high school!

"Did you know that most models are tall like you?" she asked, knowing that would get my attention. She understood me so well, which was why she also knew the right seeds to plant in order to grow my confidence.

Of course I knew models were tall, but to associate my height with *their* height? Wow! That afternoon turned out to be a wonderful day for me. My aunt, whom I loved and respected, told me I was a beautiful girl and that I could be anything I wanted to be. I could be a model! To this day, I appreciate how Aunt Rachel took me under her wing at that very crucial period of my life.

※

The next time I talked to my mother, I told her I wanted to be a model. That was the first time I ever revealed to her my dreams and aspirations. She said merely, "We have a house to move into tomorrow."

Her response was bittersweet. Bitter because she was so busy providing for us through her job as a medical transcriber that she didn't leave time for me, with all my dreams and needs; sweet because her news of a house meant we were finally moving out of Ann Lee's. And though a house was great, I wanted her to acknowledge the fact that I wanted to model. Her lack of response corroborated my fears that I wasn't pretty enough.

No big deal that she felt that way about me, I told myself. No big deal.

※

My sister Rece and I gladly moved out of Ann Lee's house and into a two-bedroom rental back in San Pablo, California, the town where I was born. I was glad, in spite of the fact that we had very few belongings to furnish our home.

Our new house greeted us with cold emptiness. We grinned anyway; Rece and I and entrenched ourselves in fierce gladness. Darkness overwhelmed what little light attempted to sneak in through the blinds. We had no light bulbs. After several hours of moving and unpacking things, gladness wore off and hunger settled in. Without any food in the cupboards, being glad was just too challenging.

That evening around six-thirty, my mother left us there while she ran to the store. She returned with a box of Fruit Loops, a quart of milk, one plastic bowl, a package of plastic spoons and some light bulbs. My little sister ate first, then me, then my mother. I sat on a mattress on the floor with tears welling up in my eyes, but I refused to let them fall. Rece sniffled throughout the night. At age nine, she was still fragile over our separation from our father. That first night in our new house was tough. So tough that I actually longed for life at Ann Lee's. At least she had food.

※�※

The hidden blessing behind our move was that we opened this new chapter in our lives a little closer to my father's parents in Richmond. They extended an invitation for us to visit them whenever we wanted. My grandmother and uncle both played the piano. My grandparents paid for me to take piano lessons at a studio near their house. Excited with this news, I dreamed of becoming the next Liberace as well as a world-famous dancer.

Every Saturday morning, my mother would drop us off at my grandparents' house on her way to work. My grandfather took me to and from my piano lessons and, later in the day, I would lie across my grandparents' bed, reading their *Jet* and *Ebony* magazines. The black men and women in those magazines intrigued me.

During one routine Saturday date with their *Ebony* magazine, I pointed to the fashion section showcasing the models and declared, "That's what I want to do."

"Oh, you would be a *beautiful* model," my grandmother told me with enthusiasm and assurance. "You're tall and pretty too."

"Do you really think so?" I believed and doubted her at the same time.

"Yes!" she exclaimed, "Just ask your grandfather."

I looked over at my grandfather who sprawled in his usual spot—an oversized chair near the foot of the bed—munching on peanuts in the shell. He loved peanuts. I loved him. He exuded such calm and warmth that I loved being around him. How my father—with all his evil ways—could be this man's and woman's son, will always be a mystery to me.

With a big grin, Grandpa praised, "Yep, you're the prettiest lil' thing!"

I grinned back with delight. I felt safe. I felt like I'd be okay. "I want to be a television broadcaster, too," I blurted out before I even knew the words were on my tongue. I was obviously on a roll with my ambitions. "And I want to have a talk show." Why stop now with the dreams, right? And besides, someday Oprah would come along and show everybody that it could be done.

So there, I'd said it. All my cards were on the table. I aspired to be a model, a television broadcaster and a talk show host. I had finally achieved some focus in life. I returned to gazing at the large, glossy pages of the magazine. I was hooked.

⚜

Later at home, I took a chance and told my mother about my newfound ambitions. This time she actually listened, and a week later, she enrolled me in one of the most popular modeling schools in San Francisco. The ball finally began to roll! All of a sudden, my mother cared about my dreams.

To this day, I remember how excited I was at the prospect of modeling classes. I told everyone I knew about my new journey. One cousin looked at me and chided, "You ain't gonna be s***!" Another non-believer! Just more fuel for my desire to achieve my goals.

I would laugh about it one day. Boy, would I show him!

BE-You-TIFUL
TRINITY

Friendly Fear
PRACTICAL APPLICATION

When we're afraid, we often run or hide. However, fear has become my friend. I've learned to smile in its face, because I know every time it knocks at my door, it provides an opportunity for me to grow.

As children, we are taught *fear of all the wrong things, for all the wrong reasons.* Children are fearless until an adult brainwashes them into believing there's something to be afraid of. Our parents instill in us fear of the things they're afraid of—often without meaning to.

I was afraid to admit that I wanted to be a successful model and talk show host. I believed that I was a nobody because my father treated the whole family as if we were nobodies. I believed that I was not worth the effort it took to educate me because no one in my family valued learning.

As odd as it sounds, *I was afraid of being me.*

Using the Fear Factor

When you find yourself in awkward and fearful places, do not make excuses for your fear. Instead, remember this Fear Factor Trinity:

1.   **Identify the fear factor.** Ask: What am I afraid of and why?

2.   **Make fear your closest friend.** Once you identify the source of fear, redirect the negative energy into positive growth with these affirmations:

- *Friendly fear can Motivate me.* Friendly fear motivated me to be a better model, commentator and speaker. Once I knew my fear and faced it, I could use it as a ladder to get to the next level of success.
- *Reverent fear will Instruct me.* Reverent fear ordered my steps. I believe that God is the only One who can show me the right path to take, and that the reverent fear of God is the beginning of wisdom.
- *Cautious fear should Focus me.* Cautious fear encouraged me to think and pray before I moved to make a decision.

3.   Prepare for your purpose and *rise above your fears.* Being able to manipulate fear requires preparation. The times I had to perform in a huge show and found myself utterly terrified (and I do mean *terrified,* not just nervous), it was because I was *not prepared for the fear factor.* I did not do what I should have done to perform 100%. Whatever your goals are in life, remember: *success is only revealed in sweat, and not in regret. You* must pay the price. When you practice and prepare there is *no room for fear.*

Remember: *Success does not come easily—it takes hard work.*

CHAPTER FOUR

Growing Pains

BY THE TIME I REACHED FOURTEEN—A TOWERING FOURTEEN, at five feet, eleven inches—I really *did* look like a giraffe in comparison to my friends. No other girl—worse yet, no other *student*—in my whole school stood taller than me. I absolutely *hated* it. I was even more compelled to study successful models. I loved Naomi Campbell and Tyra Banks, but Cindy Crawford was my favorite. All of them were tall. I was tall. All of them had long, thin legs. I had long, thin legs. I was perfect for modeling. I could finally see it!

Fashion shows were rarely televised before the advent of the Style Channel. As an alternative, I keenly studied magazine models: their look, their poise, their attitude.

Modeling is all about attitude.

These women had a perfected look that made them seem like alien creatures. How could a mere high school girl relate to anything that perfect? It intimidated me...and it challenged me, stirring up my determination to make myself beautiful like them. Only later in life did I discover that those magazine models' perfection was owing to the almighty airbrush.

Despite the fact that I knew the glossy perfection of the model was as illusory as a magician's trick, modeling became my whole world. It permeated my thoughts almost every minute of the day. I experimented with make-up and different looks. I learned about Sam Fine, the make-up artist with the magic touch. I started dreaming about meeting him someday so that he could turn my "mug" into the life mask of a beautiful African

Goddess—Nefertiti the Second. I wanted him to capture my strongest features, as he had done with all his other "projects," turning average-looking girls into queens.

⚜

I never completed that modeling course, although it really didn't matter. They kept asking for more and more money—money that my mother just didn't have. In hindsight, I realize that the purpose of that modeling school in my life was not to benefit me in modeling (it was overpriced, and I can't even tell you one thing I learned there), but as a key instrument in giving me back my momma. For the first time in my life, my mother seemed to really care about me; she put her hard-earned money into helping me launch my dream.

I began to understand that my mother really *did* love us, and cared about our aspirations, but was simply overwhelmed with the responsibility of being the sole provider—a job that should have been shared by my father. It wasn't until later in life that I learned this. What my mother went through all those years with (and without) my dad and how deeply she felt the emotional scars of his abandonment is unfathomable. Even today, my heart bleeds with compassion when I recall how hard she worked at making a life for Rece and me. My mother, and all those other women and men in the world who have stepped up to the challenge of raising their children alone, deserve to be celebrated.

As I matured, I learned something that helped me overcome my resentment toward my mother: No one is perfect. We all make mistakes. When I accepted that instead of insisting on perfection in other people, my momma became my idol.

⚜

When I was fifteen, we moved from San Pablo to Vallejo, California. Once again, a new house, a new school and new friends; still no father. This time, though, getting acquainted didn't seem so bad. I tried out for the dance team and made it. It's funny how being on some sort of high school team— whether it's basketball, cheerleading, band or flag football—always helps to get you accepted by the "in" crowd. My life began to feel normal—that is, aside from my haunting memories.

And then there was Richard, my mother's boyfriend who eventually moved in with us. I liked Richard...but then again, I *didn't* like Richard. I *liked* Richard because he attended all of my basketball games when I was in Junior High back in Rodeo. He also took my friends and I to the Golden State Warriors' games. Even though the Warriors were awful at that time, we went just to get a glimpse of the super-star players on opposing teams—especially Lakers, Bulls and Celtics.

On the other hand, I *didn't* like Richard because he got my mother's attention at a time when I felt it should belong to Rece and me. Sometimes, though, I thought it would be cool for him to take over my father's role for everyone's sake. After all, he adequately represented the father figure we never had; doing things for us that my real father had never done and would never consider doing.

But deep inside, I still loved my father. Funny, isn't it? I even secretly hoped that someday he would transform into a nice, normal dad, anxious to return to his family–to love them, protect them and provide for them. I always did dream big.

🙪

In celebration of my sixteenth birthday, Richard took my sister, mother and I out to dinner. During the main course, he asked me what I planned to do after high school. Instead of my stock answer, "Modeling," this time I said, "Television broadcasting."

"What happened to modeling?" my mother asked, looking perplexed.

My sister stopped eating and stared in anticipation of my answer as well. She had never heard me speak about anything as much, and as passionately, as I did about being a model. I'm sure I bored her to tears.

"I'm not pretty enough," I shyly replied. As I looked at everyone's eyes fixed on me, a dam of frustration broke, giving way to a flood of tears. I hid my face in my napkin and cried.

Richard, embarrassed for having initiated this landslide of emotions, tried his best to console me by putting his arm around me.

"I don't really know what I want to be!" I confessed, blurting out each syllable between sobs.

I felt confused, alone, unsure of so much. While some of my classmates had already begun their search for scholarships in desirable schools, I didn't even know what I wanted to study, let alone where to study it.

Because I didn't know how to pick a school, my selection process would involve a series of best guesses. I needed someone to guide me. I wanted someone to take charge of my life, to show me what I should do. *I certainly didn't know.*

Richard cared enough to take up that task. The next day, through a personal connection, he set up an appointment for me with a modeling agency in nearby Walnut Creek. They assigned me to a fashion show at a spectacular winery in Sonoma Valley. My mother graciously rented a car for me to get to and from the rehearsal and show. I proudly told all my friends about my first job and, to my surprise, they seemed genuinely happy for me—I was suddenly *cool.* They threw a million questions my way. I didn't have too much information, so I made up most of my answers. After all, that was the most attention I'd ever gotten from them—positive attention that is—and there was no guarantee it would happen again.

꧁꧂

The following school year, my senior year, I earned the title "Most Beautiful Girl" of our senior class. When I received news of that, I thought I would faint right on the spot. *How could this be? How in the world could I, who was "ugly as my momma," be voted "most beautiful" among my peers?*

As the reality of it sank in, my classmates' approval felt especially good. I took my model's strut on cloud nine. Deep down, I continued to doubt my beauty, but decided to go ahead, look confident on the outside and enjoy the attention, just as I enjoyed the attention with my modeling job.

The "Most Beautiful Girl" award was a picture of me in the yearbook as one of the class notables. The night before picture day, excitement and anxiety robbed me of a good night's sleep. In the morning, with dark circles under my eyes, I chose my favorite blue sweater with a mock turtleneck. Previous moments of elation turned into pure frustration when my so-called favorite outfit suddenly did not compliment me well and my hair decided to have an epic "bad hair" day.

One of the most gratifying moments of my life lay just ahead, and I looked *awful.* Needless to say, in my opinion, the picture in the yearbook looked more like the "Most Okay-Looking Girl" of our senior class.

And that, friends, is exactly how low self-esteem operates. The mind takes a compliment—a positive situation—and turns it into an ordeal. The heart begins to doubt, the lips begin to speak that doubt and the mind wallows in disbelief. As a result, dreams are squelched and goals (if even considered) are only set within one's comfort zones. Score another point for low self-esteem and for all the naysayers that put it where it would do the most harm.

In order for me to win that constant battle raging in my mind between the positive and the negative, I had to fervently believe in my heart all the things I wanted to happen. I had to keep believing them against all odds.

Believing was a small yet vital step that once taken, would pave the way for those big leaps of faith to come.

BE-You-TIFUL
TRINITY

Planted Seeds
PRACTICAL APPLICATION

I've said before that words are powerful. Words can enable or disable us. Words are like seeds planted deep in the soil of our souls. The person who captures our ear can often manipulate our heart.

A gardener plants a tiny seed to produce an apple tree. However, with the proper nurturing, it will grow into a large tree that bears fruit. When the seed is planted in the ground, it may take some time for it to take root. After the seed is rooted in the earth, it must push through the soil and dirt to begin the visible growth process. The gardener believes and later *knows* as the weeks go by, that the tree will grow and that someday it will put out blossoms and bear fruit. If the seeds are good, the tree will produce good fruit; if they're bad, the tree can't help but produce bad fruit.

It's the same with words. The words that were planted in me as a child grew into fear, bitterness and hatred. Years later, when it was time for me to step out to engage in my purpose, those disabling words overshadowed my reality. Even though I was voted "Most Beautiful Girl" in my school, I could not accept that. I was crippled by my past, paralyzed by those words.

So, my quest became to uproot the negative roots of fear, insecurity, uncertainty, bitterness and hatred, and to nurture the positive seeds of confidence, certitude and love.

Gardening for Growth

Here are a trio of "gardening" tools that I've found helpful in this process:

1. **Get your shovel.** It's time to dig deep. Many of us are reluctant to dig deep because we're afraid of what we'll find. Once we expose our problems, we must uproot them. There are three steps to doing this:

- Get underneath your issues. *What has stunted your growth? Be specific.*
- What should go or stay? *Who or what has caused the greatest pain in your life?*
- Inspect for weeds. *What issues have surfaced in your life that challenge your quest to be you?*

2. **Take out your hoe.** Prepare new ground. After we dig up old roots (the past) we need to replace them with new seeds, which means the soil of our hearts must be tilled and prepared for new growth.

- Replace old thoughts, behaviors and people with new ones.
- After identifying the negative seeds of words and images, guard your surroundings so that these negative influences don't begin surfacing again.
- The key to producing growth will be your consistency in keeping a watchful eye on your progress.

3. **Get out your watering pot.** It is time to water and feed the newly planted seeds of success. The truth of God's Word is the best food and water for healthy growth.

CHAPTER FIVE

Hope

UPON GRADUATION FROM HIGH SCHOOL, MY modeling career began to blossom. During that same time, my mother's love life began to wither. She and Richard went their separate ways. I assumed that he simply found another woman—a common behavior of men, from my point-of-view. Having relied on Richard's salary to help make ends meet, once again, my mother, sister and I were thrust into the dreaded insecurity of having to find a place to lay our heads.

My opinion of men dropped another notch. I was too young to really know any better, but experienced enough in anguish to form a distorted opinion of men: *none* of them were dependable—not one. I also concluded that at some point in my life, if I were stupid enough to let a man in, he would just walk out again.

By this time, my modeling assignments were steady, but my earnings were not enough to help support us; therefore, we humbled ourselves yet again and moved in with my godmother, Claudette Hamilton, known to most people as "Mom." Mom had given birth to only two daughters and a son of her own; yet through legal adoption of some and spiritual adoption of many, a great number of children—all of whom wished they had been born into her family—used that term of endearment.

So after all my years of yearning and praying for a *real* family—a fully equipped family with loving parents and as much normalcy as humanly possible—God answered my prayers by sending me Mom. A powerful woman of God, she became the strongest spiritual force in my life.

Mom scared me at times with her bold prayers, public dialogues with God and her rock-solid certainty about the outcome of certain things if people did or did not do what the Bible said was right. Well, maybe "scared" isn't quite the right word—not with the wonderment of it all. I was just scared of how little I knew about faith compared to Mom. Sitting in church pews all my life did nothing to clear up my confusion about religion. Only much later did I discover that it's not religion, as such, that simplifies life, it's having a *relationship* with God. That's what freed me from the bondage of confusion and brought me back to life.

I guess as much as I wanted Mom's spiritual confidence to rub off on me, I doubted I'd know what to do with it once I had it. I had only the dawning conviction that, no matter how much I suffered, the Lord was watching over me from Heaven, and that He'd sent Mom as my guardian angel to watch over me here on Earth.

Mom's duties as a guardian angel actually started way back in the early days of my father's fits of rage. She and my momma had known each other for years. I don't remember how they met; but to hear them tell it, they'd bonded instantly.

I believe my mother secretly looked for some of Mom's spiritual confidence to rub off on her as well. Any kind of confidence, in my opinion, would have helped Momma to escape my father's wrath. But it never came—neither from Mom nor from perseverance on my mother's part. So Mom simply radiated enough boldness for both of them. As fearless and as quick as Wonder Woman herself, Mom would appear at our house when beckoned, ready to save us from the villain of the piece.

On one such occasion, my doped-up father stormed into the house—probably returning from an evening rendezvous with one of his girlfriends—greeting my mother with a slap in the face and spitting obscenities at her. Momma rarely called for help—just took the beatings as though she deserved them. But this particular night, she called Mom.

As soon as Rece and I heard Mom's tires screech in the driveway, we darted to open the front door. She'd come straight from bed, clad in an old nightgown and one slipper. It still looked like a red, white and blue Wonder Woman costume to these eyes.

Restraining my father came easy for Mom. I don't remember how she did it, but it seemed as though God, Himself walked into the room and got in my daddy's face. Mom's authority just worked that way—the combination of a sweet, calming voice, mixed with a strong, brave spirit.

⚜

Mom was not the only one in her household who displayed such exemplary character—her three children graciously shared her with so many others, especially Rece and me. Her two daughters took us under their wings too. We loved them dearly for that. Only a few years older than us, they sensed our lack of maturity about life's matters and stepped in to fill the gaps in our understanding.

Mom rescued us many times and in many ways, whenever we called on her. However, not until the summer of my eighteenth birthday, while living with her, did she slide into the driver's seat of my life. She believed in me and declared that I'd do great things, long before I could believe it myself. Mom became more than just a godmother. She morphed into a magic carpet; lifting my dreams and me up, up and away.

⚜

Things were working out well for me with modeling, so I should have been content. But I wasn't, and I couldn't pretend to be. I only had it together on the *outside*; on the *inside*, trouble brewed. My spirit was uneasy, hungry—something was still lacking.

Modeling may have been my first job, but public speaking remained my first love. I took pleasure in talking if I thought it might make a difference in someone else's life. Soon after moving in with Mom, opportunities came my way to do just that. Not paid opportunities, but volunteer ones, where I gave hope and made a difference, as Mom was doing with me every day.

I taught Sunday school classes for elementary school children and worked with younger teens in the community. No matter how much I thought of myself as a messed-up kid, those children suffered more than I ever had. Their issues of abuse, hunger and neglect made my insecurities seem trivial.

"Ms. Jada, you got anything to eat?" I rarely entered a room without hearing that from one or more of them. They all looked hungry. They all acted hungry. And in truth, they were...all the time. When Mom served them snacks, they beamed with the contentment that only comes with a full belly.

I swore to myself that if I ever acquired serious money, I would feed hungry children everywhere I could. I'd been in their shoes—not sure when and if my next meal would come—but I had no money at all back then. Living in someone else's home with barely a penny to my name meant I had only hope and attention to give—which I learned was just as valuable to their futures as food.

The way I looked at it, God, in His grace, had given me Mom, who showered me with attention and hope when I'd needed it most. Therefore, I had to pass that same gift on to others.

※

I continued teaching the children for a few years after entering Contra Costa College in San Pablo to study English and Communications. After my second year there, I participated in an internship at WILD 107, the hottest radio station in the San Francisco Bay Area, learning voiceovers and commercials. I intently and proficiently gained inside knowledge of the workings of the radio world—a perfect way to help fulfill one of my life's desires to be a radio personality. I devoured information during my time at the station, amazing even myself with my adeptness at voiceovers and commercials.

The super-hot DJ I worked with once complimented me on a commercial that I produced.

"Really?" was the only response to his praise that I could muster in my moment of shock. *Wow!* I thought later, *Here's something else I'm good at besides modeling and dancing.*

I allowed myself to be encouraged by that discovery. Inspiration from people in authority—as small a thing as it may seem—was a key motivational factor in my climb to success.

※

After one year of interning, an opportunity to travel with Mom presented itself, drawing me away from my studies. Mom involved herself heavily in youth conferences, which required her to be on the road for periods of time. I figured a temporary break from school would be okay. Little did I know that attending just a few workshops and conferences would evolve into three years of constant activity.

Observing Mom's expertise in the areas of music, coordinating plays and teaching spiritual principles to thousands of young people prepared me to deliver "mini" messages of my own at those conferences from time to time. I did so with heartfelt confidence, thanks to her.

Mom instilled hope in me, pushing me to fully explore my talents and interests. Like a careful gardener, she fed my passion, dreams and most importantly, self-identity so that it blossomed according to her great expectations for me. Left to my own devices, I surely wouldn't have figured it out. Before Mom, I often felt like that little silver, metal ball in a pinball machine—ricocheting here and there, clamoring to and fro; all at someone else's whim.

⚶

One summer a promising opportunity to promote our music ministry was presented to Mom and those of us who ministered with her. There was a lot involved; including a move to *Music City*, USA: Nashville, Tennessee. Hard as it was to leave our California roots, we all felt compelled to do so.

Nashville, with its beautiful rolling hills and Appalachian mountain dialect, presented quite an initial culture shock for me and my sister. For two "Valley Girls" planted in the middle of "Hillbilly" country, adjusting to the move was a challenge.

After months of dedication and hard work, the promises that had beckoned us twenty-four hundred miles from home fell short. Everyone participating in the endeavor sustained major disappointment, but we chalked it up to one great learning experience. Mom and Momma decided that we would remain there, nonetheless, to see what else Tennessee had to offer.

Two of the greatest lessons I learned during that "hit-or-miss" exploration: never give up, and never take "no" for a final answer. During those years on the road with Mom, I never gave up on my dream of modeling. It just stood by patiently, waiting for me to pick it up once again.

BE-You-TIFUL
TRINITY

Mentoring: What Everyone Needs
PRACTICAL APPLICATION

Remember, the most successful people wouldn't be where they are in life if it wasn't for *great mentorship*. We should never put our talents and abilities above leadership and guidance. Accountability, humility and good mentorship are the keys to success. God purposely puts those keys within our grasp—we have only to reach out and take them.

When I was a child, I longed for the love and guidance of my mother and father. But later I learned to accept the support of others who pushed and motivated me. I also learned not to become attached to those who merely tolerated me.

I couldn't rely on my mother and father for guidance, so God gave me my godmother, Mom, as a mentor. I knew she was my mentor when she confirmed the plan that God had already revealed to me, and took practical steps to put my feet on that path.

Never take for granted the importance of a mentor; God reveals Himself, instructs us and directs us through good mentors.

Ah, but didn't I warn you about patterning yourself on someone else's design and emulating them? Yes, I did. There will be plenty of people in your life who will try to control you, manipulate you or make your decisions for you, but a true mentor is different.

True Mentor Checklist

There are, as you've no doubt guessed, a trinity of things a true mentor does to help you become YOU.

1.   They recognize, make plain and communicate to you your *true purpose* in life. They do this by speaking to the *potential* in you and overlooking the *struggles* within you.

2.   They never *invalidate* you, but always seek to find a way to *uphold* you. They do this by *strengthening* your weakness, *destroying* your pride and *rebuilding* your confidence. This means they give you what you *need,* not necessarily what you *want.*

3.   They don't become your best friend or rely on your feedback and praise to stay committed to helping you. All they need is your *commitment* to them.

CHAPTER SIX

Humble Beginnings

As much as I loved broadcasting, and as energized as I became when speaking in front of an audience, my inner spirit told me it was time to put modeling back on the front burner. With the window of opportunity for modeling being so small in comparison to broadcasting, I felt a sudden urgency to seriously focus on modeling right away, right there in Nashville.

Now I admit, I couldn't imagine Nashville offering me anything in the way of fashion modeling; but nonetheless, I worked out regularly, building a toned and sculpted body…and a craving for the runway. I diligently prepared—mentally and physically—for my modeling career. No college degree was required for what I would be doing. In fact, I wouldn't need much education at all—just height, poise, and beauty. They told me I had all that. So I prepared myself, intending to reach the top, though the path leading there was anything but clear. One thing *was* clear, though, broadcasting would have to wait.

One day, while working out at the YMCA in Nashville, I met a lovely lady named Sherry. She asked me if I had ever modeled.

"A little," I modestly replied.

"You are absolutely beautiful," she marveled. "Here's my card. I own a modeling agency nearby and I would love for you to come in and see me."

A few days later, I called and set up an appointment to visit Sherry's agency. From the moment I walked into the office, people bombarded me with kindness. I liked Sherry. Not only was she pretty, but she took an interest in me; I appreciated that.

As I look back on that first visit, I laugh at how she gave me the "once over" while I was seated across from her desk. At that time, my long black hair cascaded over my shoulders, and the first thing she asked was, "Is that your real hair?"

"Yes," I answered with a little indignation in my voice. I wasn't used to anyone being so blunt. She offered no apology for asking, just scrawled notes on her pad for each observation she made.

"Smile," she said, gritting her teeth as an example. "I want to see your teeth."

I offered a genuine smile.

"Pretty smile. You need to arch your brows, though," she said matter-of-factly, as she pondered the rest of my face. "How tall are you?"

"Five-foot-eleven," I answered—proudly now.

"Stand up so I can take your measurements."

I slipped out of my coat, stood up and stared straight ahead. Over all, I wasn't offended—just glad that she considered putting me to work.

When she finished measuring me, Sherry gave me the phone number of a photographer to call to get a composite card made. The "comp card"— which consists of the model's name, photos and measurements—is the most basic, essential tool for a model. I followed her orders and immediately made an appointment with the photographer.

The very next day, Sherry called. She asked if I'd called the photographer yet. I told her I had. She then granted me an assignment at a department store. I truly believe that had I answered "No," she wouldn't have been so quick to send me to that photo shoot. I realized right then that obedience and readiness would take me far in this industry.

I immediately fell in love with the whole thing—the photo shoots, the runway shows, the traveling, the attention—everything! I quickly mastered the fine art of walking in four to five inch heels. Sherry continued to send work my way. I worked so much that I became a pro in no time. I challenged myself to not be a merely good runway model, but to achieve the status of the next up-and-coming supermodel.

✄

From Nashville, I returned to San Francisco to live for a short period of time, signing with *Stars, The Agency*. And as if being back in familiar territory wasn't thrilling enough for me, I had the experience of a lifetime there:

my very first Oscar de la Renta fashion show! I was so proud to be chosen from the many who auditioned.

Even though I had quite a few fashion shows under my belt by now, nothing thus far prepared me for what happened next. On the day of the fitting for the show, approximately thirty girls were shoved into a sparsely decorated room like a herd of two-legged cattle. A thick, metal door separated us from the show's crew, who were busying themselves with last-minute details. Not familiar with this protocol, I stood with grave anticipation. Everyone watched everyone else, "sizing" each other up.

The air-conditioning in that cramped space was minimal at best, and I began to sweat like a horse. This was not the time to lose my cool. I needed to sit down, but instead I stood—mesmerized by twenty-nine of the most beautiful women I had ever seen in real life. Their flawless faces and bodies could have easily graced the pages of *Vogue* and *Cosmopolitan*.

My breathing accelerated as perspiration beaded on my skin. I wanted to sit but feared moving, not wanting to draw attention to myself. *What am I doing here?* I thought. These models were professionals—some chatted about flying from Paris to New York, some from Miami to San Francisco and others from Milan to Los Angeles. I wasn't a professional—not yet.

A couple of the models were fluent in French and flaunted their knowledge about how the French hated models who could not speak their language. The more these girls boasted of their experiences, the less adequate I felt. Looking intently around the room, I actually recognized a few faces from commercials and print ads.

I made up my mind to just leave and lie to my agent about a sudden emergency. As I worked up the courage and will to move, the door flew open and a short, thin dark-haired man hurled himself into the room, barking orders.

"Okay, ladies! Strip!" he yelled with two claps to accent his words.

Strip? I thought, *What the heck is he talking about? He's got to be kidding!*

I could not believe it. The models immediately began to take off their clothes—no questions asked—business as usual. I began to wonder if there would be an immediate replacement for the clothes that I had to shed. That answer came quickly, as a room full of thong-clad beauties were then told to stand in line for evaluations. Every straight man on the face of this earth would have loved to be in the shoes of that little dictator. It was a meat market, but the man in charge gave no sexual regard to all the "T & A" in front of him.

Within minutes, a group of Oscar de la Renta representatives came in, looked us up and down and decided who would wear what. The opening garment was granted to the very tall, thin girl who'd bragged of flying from Paris, where she'd worked for *Fashion Week*. The man ordered her to walk. She strutted flawlessly—so poised and confident.

Fear crept over me like invisible ants. My mind kept telling me I wasn't good enough to be in that room. I prayed I didn't look as scared as I felt.

Garment after garment passed through a series of hands. I was among the last few to receive a piece. This allowed my mind more time to come up with further reasons why I should just walk out: *They don't like me. I'm too ugly. Maybe I'm too fat. I'm not as thin as the other girls. My boobs are too big. My thighs are too thick.*

But I didn't walk out.

An amazing animal-print gown finally found its way to my sweaty hands. I contained my excitement so as not to look like an amateur. With the aid of the wardrobe assistant, I wiggled into the dress. Ignoring the snugness of this silk faille around my thigh and butt area was not an option. We tugged here and there on it, which only caused more resistance by the ultra-expensive fabric.

All of a sudden the assistant yelled out, "She's too big for this one!" She turned back to me with a look of shame, "Take it off, honey."

I thought to myself, *That's what you get, thinking you belonged here. Quick, hide! Better yet, run!* My mind's solution to problems all my life had been to run and hide, and all my life, I answered myself with, *Where?*

Thin described me best—too thin by most people's standards. My childhood was riddled with skinny jokes and jabs. Yet now it was implied that I wasn't thin enough. Talk about being messed-up in the head! At five-feet-eleven, one-hundred-thirty pounds, I was *fat. Welcome to the world of modeling.*

They found a series of outfits that fit, but I still left that fitting in a state of depression and confusion. I mentally replayed the humiliation of standing in a line of thirty naked women, feeling like a piece of meat. A fat piece of meat, at that. I tried hard to block out the negativity; after all, being chosen for an Oscar de la Renta show was no small feat, especially for a new model.

The following day, I would perform in the biggest show of my career thus far, and self-confidence was nowhere to be found. I hated that feeling, but it possessed me just the same.

Modeling is a lifetime of rejection—the kind of painful rejection that can destroy your self-esteem if you're not careful. The last thing I needed was to feel "less than," so I fought through the pain, ignored any rejection and made a conscious effort to flaunt my good qualities. Simply put, to achieve success in modeling—or anything, for that matter—one must recognize her strengths and go for it, full-speed ahead.

※

The following afternoon, I underwent the magic of the make-up artist, wondering—only for a moment—if he, too, thought I was fat. Minutes after the transformation, we were into our first outfits and the show began. What an incredible experience!

Mr. de la Renta planted himself front and center. I glanced at him every time I walked the runway. The audience applauded generously when I styled a sexy micro-mini skirt with sleek, thigh high boots.

I strutted my butt off that day, giving one-hundred-and-ten percent. I *loved* the runway, and the runway loved me. It proved the one place where security and self-assurance reigned for me. I excelled at it and knew it…most of the time. But there were still moments…

As the show drew to a close, Mr. de la Renta stood up, turned to the audience and apologized for displaying his work on overweight models. *Did I just hear what I thought I heard?* I wanted to die. Oh, I knew he wasn't referring to me specifically, but standing there, in front of an audience, I suddenly felt all boobs and thighs.

The audience laughed, so I suppose he was just kidding, but I was warned. Rejection you ignore, but criticism (particularly constructive criticism) you take, without offense, and turn it around for good. Immediately after that show, I changed my eating habits; I ate only chicken, turkey and salads. Before long, I clambered down to a svelte one-hundred-twenty-three pounds—a perfect modeling weight for me.

※

After that show, I was unstoppable. Obedience paid off for me. I obeyed the obvious signs that I needed to lose weight and I did it safely, but with haste. At my new weight, I auditioned for lots of fashion shows and booked about ninety-five percent of them. Most were in the Bay Area; none were in New York. I longed to go to New York. That was the true test for a model. I dreamed about it, but that was about it; I was too unsure of it all, I suppose, to really pursue it.

I had heard all kinds of terrifying stories about young models compromising themselves in order to make it in the Big Apple. One girl left San Francisco when she was only fifteen years old and settled into a New York apartment, sponsored by an agency. Three months later, after refusing to sleep with the female owner of the agency, the girl was kicked out. With nowhere to go, she sold her body to earn enough money to fly back to the West Coast. So many of those kinds of stories surfaced and terrified me that I did not want to leave San Francisco.

However, one success story always kept me hopeful. While training with a major agency in San Francisco, I worked with a model named Christie Turlington. Christie and I shared the honor of studying under long-time model trainer, Jimmy Grimme. I am forever indebted to Mr. Grimme for teaching me not just how to walk, but how to walk with Attitude.

Not too long after we met, Christie got an opportunity to go to New York and took it. Before long, she was one of the best-known faces in the modeling industry. She made the cover of almost every magazine that graced the grocery store checkout stands; not to mention department store ads and runways from New York to Milan. I was so proud that Christie succeeded. Most are not as fortunate.

I refused the thought of failure. I refused to get to New York only to have to sell my body to buy a plane ticket home. Christie's story gave me inspiration. I decided right then and there that where I went was not as important as *how* I went. So I would go victoriously!

BE-**You**-TIFUL
TRINITY

Positive Pain
PRACTICAL APPLICATION

Uncertainty and insecurity have contributed the most to my pain. Though I was physically abused by my mother, psychologically abused by my father and sexually abused by others, I believe that the after-affects of all of those abuses are more painful than the abuse itself.

Even after following my dreams, I found that insecurity haunted me by causing me to compare myself to the other beautiful women I felt I had to compete with. I was *never* good enough!

This was my greatest pain. I would eventually have to learn to rise above it to get a clear view of my future. I believe pain should be used positively as a learning tool that pushes you upward or forward to your destiny. *Employ pain to work for you rather than you being pushed around by it.*

Be-You-Tiful "Get-over-it" Tips

Here are a trio of tips calculated to help you "get over yourself."

   1.   It is what it is. If it looks like a duck, and quacks like a duck, it's a duck. When we understand this simple principle, we can rise above pettiness. There are some things that just cannot be changed and those things don't merit our attention or focus. *We become truly powerful when we learn to spend our time and energy on things that really matter.*

   2.   It's not that deep. There are things that really hurt us, but we have to decide whether or not these things are worth agonizing over. The measure of our success depends on what situations we deem important enough to tackle. *Remember, a hurt is only as deep as you choose to probe and dig.*

3. **Whatever it takes.** What does it really take to get over hurt and pain? Ignore pain! Don't feed it energy. It doesn't deserve a response or access to the inner you.

CHAPTER SEVEN

My New Season!

STILL WORKING THE SAN FRANCISCO CIRCUIT, I evolved into a strong runway model and promoted myself as such. In the spring of 1999, I met a model who told me about the *Ebony Fashion Fair*. The *Ebony Fashion Fair* began in 1956 as an offspring of *Ebony Magazine*, the world's premier Black magazine.

Noted as the world's largest traveling fashion show, *Ebony Fashion Fair* travels today to nearly one hundred-eighty cities worldwide. Each show features approximately two hundred ultra-flamboyant ensembles from the fashion capitals of the world—including Paris, Milan, Rome, London, New York and Los Angeles.

Prior to learning that, I didn't know much about the shows except that, as a child, I had desired to be one of those beautiful black girls, gracing the stage in super-extravagant, ultra-elegant gowns. The images remained embedded in my mind all those years.

The model who told me about *Ebony Fashion Fair* encouraged me to send in my pictures. She said I needed a great headshot, full-length shot and a bikini shot. My comp card had all the pictures I needed, so I didn't have to spend extra money for a new photo shoot. However, I would have done it in a heartbeat if it meant an opportunity to become an *Ebony Fashion Fair* model.

I quickly sent my pictures to *Ebony Fashion Fair* headquarters at the Johnson Publishing Company in Chicago, Illinois. After much anticipation, I received a call telling me that I would be flown to Chicago to audition at Johnson headquarters.

I gave one-hundred-and-ten percent at that audition, and the page turned. It opened to a wonderfully new chapter in my life when I received the news of being selected for *Ebony Fashion Fair's* 1999-2000 season. Talk about excited!

I remembered that resilient eleven-year-old girl who lay on her grand-parents' bed, mentally painting herself on the shiny pages of *Ebony* magazine. That little girl didn't have to imagine it any longer, didn't have to dream about being Tyra or Naomi. Reality would put her on the pages of that magazine; reality would link her name with the likes of Tyra and Naomi.

۞

I stepped out of the cab in front of the stately Chicago Hilton on Michigan Avenue around three o'clock on a humid August afternoon. The sun did its thing in a brilliantly blue sky. Even though a large digital thermometer on one of the downtown office buildings showed a reading of only seventy-four degrees, the recent rain and high humidity made it feel like a steaming jungle. But none of that made a bit of difference to me. In fact, there could have been a summer blizzard for all I cared. The city seemed perfect—a fairytale city with glittering streets, lofty spires and perfect weather.

Loud music blared from across the street in Grant Park, downtown Chicago's most beautiful green-land and host to many of the city's free festivals—from gospel to jazz; from art to food. I watched droves of people strolling hypnotically toward the beckoning sound.

"What's going on over there?" I asked the doorman as he eagerly snatched up my bags.

"It's the annual Jazz Festival," he answered without hesitation.

My eyes lit up. I loved music, I loved dancing and I loved festivals. I wanted to go, but decided against venturing out alone just yet.

While strolling toward the front desk, I noticed about five guys in hotel uniforms hanging around the bell-stand whispering, smiling and staring at me. I shyly looked away, picking up my pace to the desk. What a strange feeling that was. I'd always desired people to notice me, but when they did, I became immediately insecure. I decided right then and there to face that demon of Insecurity, so I glanced over at the guys and flashed a smile.

One of them waved. "You one of 'dem *Ebony* models?" he blurted.

I nodded my head and continued smiling as his words evoked empowerment. He'd called me an *Ebony* model. That sounded *good!* I let it sink in for a moment: *Yes, I* am *an Ebony model! I am an Ebony model!*

What seemed like a long "runway" performance from the curbside to the front desk concluded as the young girl working the desk greeted me with, "You must be one of the *Ebony* girls." I felt like a celebrity.

I reminded myself that *Ebony* was the number one African-American magazine in the world. As a public representative of *Ebony*, I *was* a celebrity. So I gave her a big celebrity smile and responded, "Yes I am; I'm with *Ebony*, my name is Jada Jackson and I would like to check in."

As the young girl began tapping away on her computer keyboard, I glanced around, spotting two other tall, beautiful black girls chatting nearby. I figured them to be *Ebony* models as well and suddenly felt an unfamiliar sense of pride being tall, black and beautiful.

Shortly thereafter, the desk clerk handed me my room key and an envelope provided by *Ebony Fashion Fair*. The bellman and I proceeded toward the elevators.

As we walked, a security guard stopped me. "You an *Ebony* model, right?" he asked.

"Yeah."

"What's your name?"

"Jada."

"You're very pretty, Jada."

"Thank you." I was so flattered.

"Well, let me know if you need anything," he beamed. I could tell he wasn't trying to come on to me—just being nice.

I could easily get used to this. I loved Chicago already. I loved the Hilton. And I loved the staff treating me like royalty. I was in love with my new life and it was only the beginning!

An impressive and inviting room awaited me. I loved everything about it. I must have really been caught up in the moment, though, because the pungent smell of bleach and other cleaning detergents seemed as sweet to my nose as the sweet aroma of roses!

I pulled back the curtains—which matched the handsome bedspread—and took in my spectacular view of Grant Park and Lake Michigan. A sea of people graced the park with their personal lawn chairs and blankets. I couldn't remember ever being so overwhelmed with excitement. My life finally seemed worth living.

I didn't go to the festival, but continued listening to the sultry jazz waft up to my window from the park. After unpacking and making a few phone calls back home, I sat in a comfortable armchair, relishing the sunset. I accepted the fact that from this day forward, things would be different in my life!

✿

The packet of information left for us at the front desk instructed us to report to Johnson Publishing Company at nine o'clock the next morning. After eating a light breakfast, I walked the half block to the famous building, which houses the powerful operations of *Ebony* and *Jet* magazines, *Ebony Fashion Fair*, *Fashion Fair Cosmetics* and the Johnson Publishing Company Book Division.

When I arrived, four other models were already sitting on the lobby sofa. The security guard motioned for me to sign in and take a seat. After acknowledging the others with a smile and a nod, I immediately engaged in conversation with a familiar-looking model as I lowered myself to the sofa. She didn't recognize me.

"Were you at the audition?" she asked. I could see her struggling to place me.

"Yeah," I responded.

"Your hair is different," she said, seeming proud of her observation.

She was right. I'd worn my hair up in a bun for the audition, but now it was down, hanging well below my shoulders. I loved my hair, and it had finally reached a versatile length.

We congregated in the lobby until all of the models had arrived. Then, after the security guard with the sign-in sheet made a quick phone call, a short, fair-skinned lady emerged from the elevator to escort us to the seventh floor, where we would soon spend the majority of our time preparing for the show. The woman seemed rude and disconnected. She was well dressed and very pretty, but she exuded an edgy and unpleasant energy. We followed her, filing into the projection room where each of us grabbed a chair and got comfortable.

"I'm the Commentator for the *Ebony Fashion Show*," the light-skinned woman announced with obvious pride.

She then instructed us to go around the room and introduce ourselves, starting with Rodney. I remembered suave and exotic-looking Rodney from the audition. He sort of reminded me of supermodel Tyson. This was Rodney's second year, which must have been why he had a whole lot to say. His outspokenness was rather scary—I honestly didn't know a man could talk so much. The remaining introductions concluded rather quickly. Lots of different backgrounds; lots of different looks. Everyone embodied beauty in their own special way.

Having met all the models, the attention turned to the behind-the-scene movers and shakers. A robust, caramel-colored man was the assistant to the Producer—or rather the machine that kept things going. Rodney told me that this guy was a sixteen-year *Ebony Fashion Fair* veteran and accomplished designer himself, flying to Paris, Rome, Milan and New York to purchase clothes from the most famous designers in the world. He could do it with his eyes closed, Rodney confided.

The assistant producer brought in a few pieces for us to try on, quickly warning us not to get attached to them as the fittings would be intense, with clothes changing hands three or four times. I gasped at the fifty- and sixty- thousand-dollar price tags on those gowns!

⚜

The first two days started slowly, with intensity building moment-by-moment. By the third and fourth days, the routines and line-ups were in full swing. The first outfit given to me was a sexy, red, two-piece skirt-set by Gianni Molero. The top piece consisted of a tight bustier that hugged me all the way down to my navel. The bottom piece, a long, fluid skirt with a train accenting my rear, caught the wind as I walked. On the right side, a slit ran from the waistline to the floor, exposing my hip. That became my favorite piece of the entire show—it made me feel like a princess.

In fact, most of the clothes I wore made me feel like a princess. I loved them all, mainly because I just loved being an *Ebony Fashion Fair* model. Some girls, however, complained about what they wore and questioned the choice of clothing picked for them. I didn't talk much—just watched and made mental note of the different personalities.

Friday morning finally rolled around. As the morning's rehearsal got underway, the commentator came in—still exhibiting her unique blend of aloofness and arrogance—and called out, "Jada, Princess, Katrice and Candace, I need you to come with me."

I mentally retraced my actions over the past week, wondering what I might have done wrong. Thoughts of possible wrongdoing on my part intensified when we learned—while walking briskly down the hall—that Mrs. Johnson herself had summoned us. As we approached the door of her soft, flawlessly white office brought alive with glass, brass and a striking view of Lake Michigan, Mrs. Eunice Johnson welcomed us in with a polite hello in the soft accents of the South.

I stood in awe of her office décor and view. Pictures of Mrs. Johnson with some of the world's most famous designers adorned the walls. There was a pleasant aura of peace in that room that I could not articulate.

"You ladies have been chosen for the *Ebony* Magazine swimsuit photo shoot." Her words broke through my trance.

It felt like I'd died and gone to Heaven—it all seemed too good to be true! It was enough to be selected as an *Ebony Fashion Fair* model, but this—the distinction of being one of the four models in *Ebony* magazine's annual swimsuit feature! I wanted to fall down and kiss the toes of Mrs. Johnson's impeccable Gucci's in humble thanks. Imagining how ridiculous that would look, I just smiled like the others and said "Thank you."

Princess, Katrice, Candace and I were each given a bagful of swimsuits, which we modeled one at a time for Mrs. Johnson. I remember it took forever to get through all those suits; nonetheless, I savored every moment. I couldn't wait to tell my folks back home.

During lunch that day, while sharing details of our trip to Mrs. Johnson's office, Rodney jabbed, "Jada, you're so beautiful and well-spoken, I wouldn't doubt it if you got selected for that Assistant Commentator position as well."

"What?" I responded, flattered and shocked all at the same time. I didn't even know such a position was available, but didn't let on to that fact.

Immediately, thoughts raced through my head of that incredible possibility. *Me? Assistant Commentator? Why not?* But how many awesome things could I stand at once?

Walking back to the hotel after work that day, I could not help but think about what Rodney had said. I loved talking and performing. Instead of totally giving up my dream of broadcasting, commentating the shows would be an excellent opportunity to put my voice to work within the fashion environment.

Just as excitement welled up within me, like clockwork, Doubt stuck its gnarly head into the room. Doubt always starts with a question, and this time was no different. *Why would they choose you over all the other beautiful and talented models on tour?* That question demolished my excitement. *It's all Rodney's fault for talking too much,* I told myself. He'd gotten me all excited for nothing. I wanted to believe him, but me being selected for that role just didn't make sense. Just like that, there was a Smack-Down wrestling match going on in my head: Demon Doubt vs. Heavenly Hope.

As I entered the lobby of the Hilton, I saw a few of the models standing around chatting. They looked my way.

"We're going to the Bears pre-season game on Saturday; we have some free tickets. You wanna come with?" one of the guys asked, holding up a fistful of tickets.

"The Bears game?" I echoed. Of course I wanted to go...but I shouldn't. I'd had all sorts of advice from veteran models warning me that nothing came free; there always dangled a hidden price tag—that price being some booty.

I'd learned all too quickly that our "Ebony Model" title earned us access to some of the best parties, events and celebrities. Stories ran rampant about *Ebony Fashion Fair's* non-stop party days of the Seventies. Every black girl wanted to be an *Ebony Fashion Fair* model; unfortunately, sometimes not for the passion of modeling, but simply for the benefit of dating celebrities and athletes and being placed on the upper echelon's list for the hottest parties and finest restaurants.

It was possible not much had changed in the area of ulterior motives and I didn't want to find out the hard way. I wanted to stay focused on my goal, and more importantly, I *didn't* want to disappoint Mom.

"No thanks, I'll pass on the game this time; you guys have fun."

I hastened to my room and called Mom immediately to share the good news about the swimsuit feature. She sounded more excited than I was—if that was possible. It felt good to know that someone else took pride in what I did. Not that my relatives didn't, but somehow it was just different with Mom.

During my conversation, I chose to leave out what Rodney had said about the Assistant Commentator position. After all, I didn't want to get Mom's hopes up. Okay, I didn't want to get *my* hopes up.

As I prepared for bed, I prayed to God for more confidence. I had come so far; with so much at stake. I sensed that I was to build a solid foundation here, in preparation for whatever else God had in store for me. It was high time Doubt got out of Hope's way!

BE-You-TIFUL
TRINITY

Prepared for Success
PRACTICAL APPLICATION

Success demands effort, willingness, consistency and patience. When I thought of all the sleepless nights, rejections and naysayers who told me I couldn't succeed—well, didn't the very fact that I surmounted all these obstacles equal success?

Sadly, these things don't equal anything but hard times *if you don't put them into the proper perspective and then put them to use.*

There are only three things that guarantee success: God's direction, consistency and accurate mental calculations.

Spiritual Mathematics

You have to become great at mental and spiritual mathematics: adding, subtracting and multiplying things in your life.

Are you ready? Let's start calculating! Here is a trinity of Be-You-Tiful "Calculations" Tips:

ADDITION (*But seek first His kingdom and his righteousness…*)
- **Do Your Research:** Start by learning all you can about what you're passionate about. *There is no such thing as too much knowledge.* The more you know, the more you will expand and grow.

Sometimes we make careless mistakes in our calculations by unwittingly subtracting things that God may be using to help us grow. Sometimes He allows hardship and adversity so that He can add *wisdom* and *knowledge.* We should be mindful of this when we're adding it all up.

SUBTRACTION (*Watch your step!*)

- **Be Patient:** Sometimes we make the mistake of getting ahead of God's plans for us. Human vices include some patience-killers; lust, selfishness and pride among them. We think just because we get a little knowledge or have an epiphany, we're ready to go out and take on the world.

Subtracting is all about patience. We get in over our heads sometimes—especially when it comes to our careers. There is a path already set for us, but because we're impatient, we end up in the wrong place at the wrong time.

A patient person operates with *restraint* and *obedience*. If you learn how to subtract your impatience from the equation, God promises things will start adding up for you.

MULTIPLICATION (*...and all these things will be given to you, as well.*)

- **Hard Work:** After you've done your research and learned how to become humble, patient *and* you've gotten your approval from God to proceed, then it's time to work toward your purpose. One thing you have to understand about multiplication is that you'll never be able to manipulate the system to secure more for yourself. Only preparation and hard work can bring about longevity and real prosperity.

You don't have to fear losing what you've earned, but *consistency* and *honesty* will always keep you in the multiplication category.

CHAPTER EIGHT

Decisions

FINALLY, MY LIFELONG DREAM MATERIALIZED as the 1999-2000 *Ebony Fashion Fair* season got underway. Our first show opened in the suburbs of Chicago, the second Wednesday of September. Our audience might never realize the time and energy invested by so many people for the creation of the stunning and masterful showcase of the best of the best in fashion. Before any high-stepping can take place on stage—even before the models can pile onto the busses or planes—much attention is given to a grueling, meticulous, non-stop preparatory schedule.

The non-glamorous, behind-the-scenes responsibilities begin for each show when the models are presented with a number of outfits, each with matching shoes and jewelry. Each model is then equipped with a black box in which to store those shoes, jewelry and other accessories. Once those items are in the models' possession, it is their job (with the help of their assistants) to care for them—a rather intimidating task for me once I learned that some of the shoes alone cost three or four thousand dollars a pair.

A colored marking on each of the black boxes coordinates that box with one of the show's four wardrobe assistants. The assistants—one to every three or four models—doggedly tackle the packing, unpacking and care of all the garments for their designated models. It's hard to tell which presents more of a challenge to them: managing the apparel or managing the models. It's a tough job in either case.

My wardrobe assistant, Dorcas, mastered her role. I liked her as an assistant and I liked her as a person. We became very good friends. This

native Chicagoan possessed the straight-forwardness and in-your-face attitude usually reserved for the true New Yorker. However, her down-to-earth
personality made her approachable and lovable.

We had seatmates on the bus, which we were instructed could not be
our roommates. If we wanted to change roommates, it had to be done
before we went on the road. I enjoyed my seatmate, Alex, who was from
California. We had a lot in common, a lot to talk about. My assigned roommate, Dawn, requested to room with someone else. When she told me this,
I was initially offended, but understood her reasoning.

"I'd rather be with someone closer to my own age. I'm thirty-five with
a teenage daughter, so I don't think we'd have much, if anything, in common," Dawn told me simply.

Shocked to learn her age in spite of her youthful looks, I wholeheart-
edly agreed to the change. No wonder she seemed a bit standoffish! She was
almost in a different generation.

So along came Princess from Cleveland, Ohio, as my new roommate.
As a college student studying TV and Film Production, Princess had taken
a break from school to secure her ticket to Hollywood. She played her cards
right, too, because she's currently heading her own production company
with key Hollywood figures as clients.

Her extremely good looks, cappuccino-toned skin and curvaceous five-
foot-eleven frame drew immediate attention in every room she entered. Or
perhaps her effervescent personality and bubbly laughter was what really
caught everyone's attention. Either way, she had it going on. Her full curves
brought a refreshing change of scenery to the stage full of the slender, even
underfed bodies of the other models. That was one thing I really admired
about the *Ebony Fashion Fair*. The models were not super thin. They ranged
in size and skin color, showcasing diversity.

From the first time I met Princess, I accurately "sized up" her ability to
have a good time. She taught me Partying 101—not just any ole' way, but
in style! She actually learned some things from me as well, about spiritual-
ity and religion, so we ended up being a good match.

As the tour bus prepared to pull away shortly after two o'clock on that humid
afternoon of September 1999, I strove to convert all my nervous energy into
positive zeal. The blasting air-conditioning on that bus successfully battled

the sticky eighty-six degrees outside. Some native Chicagoans had it that although this was unusually warm weather for this time of year, one shouldn't complain if Indian summer delayed Chicago's notorious blustery winter winds and sub-zero temperatures.

The latecomers filed into their seats, shoving their travel bags into whatever little nook there was above them. Our business manager, Willie Davis, then gave us a heartfelt pep talk, reminding us to be grateful for the opportunity we had and not to take it for granted. Mr. Davis passed away in 2003, but his unyielding, fatherly concern and encouragement is something I'll always remember with gratitude.

After his speech, I endeavored to get lost in my thoughts—first rehashing all the past weeks' efforts; then going back further, catching another glimpse of that hope-filled eleven-year-old, lying on her grandparents' bed, flipping through *Ebony's* pages. The young girl gasped in sheer delight to discover herself on one of those pages in the most elegant gown!

🔀

I loved the energy of the audience—the "oohs" and "aahs." I drew from that energy, enjoying every minute of it. To have all eyes on me, especially while wearing a twenty-thousand-dollar gown, felt like Heaven. I fell in love with the runway every time I stepped out onto it.

The non-stop preparation before the tours was certainly anything but glamorous, and I quickly discovered that the time spent *during* the tours— particularly backstage—was no picnic either. Which was precisely why I savored every moment I spent on that runway. It became my safe haven, my fairytale come true. Yet it also served as my opportunity to reach deep down inside and pull out the greatness that had been hidden there for years.

You see, once I stepped down off that stage, the glamour was gone, the lights dimmed and the "oohs" and "aahs" were silenced. The fairytale book was closed and put away, and the greatness inside gave way to insecurity: *How did I do? Did I look breathtaking in that outfit, or awkward? Did the audience love me or even like me?* Even as people backstage told me I was terrific, gave me thumbs up and other encouraging signs, Doubt taunted me with its inane questions.

Of course, stepping down off the stage also meant stepping back into rush, rush, rush; do, do, do; go, go, go; leaving no time to listen to Doubt's nasty whispers.

※

A fashion tour schedule tests the character of even the most seasoned model—you're constantly moving; never given much of a break. *Ebony Fashion Fair* models work six days a week. Sometimes we travel for twelve to fourteen days without a single day off. But even at its toughest, it seemed well worth it to me, especially considering it was all in the name of charity. This show has raised millions of dollars for charitable organizations all over the country. It was such a pleasure meeting all of those distinguished women of sororities, like Alpha Kappa Alpha, Delta Sigma Theta and exclusive groups like Links, Incorporated and Jack and Jill of America.

On that particular tour, we started off traveling from Chicago to all its surrounding cities. We then went to Milwaukee, Columbus, Harrisburg, Hartford and Boston. We continued on to New York City, Newark, Baltimore, Richmond, D.C., Buffalo, Cleveland and Charlotte, with dozens more small towns along the way. All in all, we performed in nearly one hundred eighty cities during those nine months. We had a blast every step of the way!

Out of all the cities on our schedule, the one I looked forward to most was New York. I had never visited there, but based on all that I'd heard—specifically regarding its fashion industry—loving it would be no problem for me. As soon as we arrived, I felt the burst of energy the city's atmosphere is known to produce—so far, so good.

※

We checked in early Saturday on the executive floor of the Hilton New York Hotel. The hotel was conveniently located near Fifth Avenue shopping, Central Park and other famous landmarks. I could hardly wait until our day off on Monday to take full advantage of those attractions. While I quivered with excitement over the prospect of my first-ever shopping spree in the Big Apple, Princess eagerly planned what would be my first-ever club-hopping experience in New York's vibrant nightlife.

Going out in New York was exciting, but intimidating. Mom and Momma had both cautioned me to stay out of the clubs and most of all be careful of the guys that I chose to date. This was definitely an experimental period in my life, during which I had to make the decision to ignore or heed that loving advice. I wanted to step out on my own and experience what my peers were doing. I wanted to be free—if you can call that freedom. This was a time in my life when my Christian values and good judgment were put to the test like never before.

Our escort for the night would be Princess' boyfriend, a former Cleveland Browns football player. He was scheduled to meet us at our hotel room around eight o'clock that evening.

"Is it okay if he comes up to the room?" Princess asked me as we followed the bellman to our room. Without even waiting for my response, she continued, "He's bringing one of his friends along for you to meet."

"Yeah, sure, I guess it's okay," I said with some hesitation. Actually, men in my hotel room was *not* okay.

Truthfully, I'd never ventured out to *any* nightclubs before, so being introduced to the best of them would really be a treat. Partying had just never fit into my lifestyle. That was about to change.

※

My initiation to New York City was fabulous. There was some quick sightseeing, delicious cuisine and of course, tons of window-shopping. Having lived with Mom not too long ago with nothing to call my own, I was a fairly conservative shopper. Therefore, most of the thrill came from just being in the stores and specialty boutiques, not so much from buying things.

The day quickly gave way to our nighttime excursion. I prepared for the evening by putting on a skimpy little black camisole I purchased at a boutique on Fifth Avenue. My tight-fitting jeans and black sandals with three-inch heels complimented the camisole quite well, as did my impeccable makeup job. When away from the stage, I preferred makeup applied moderately, yet with enough flair to radiantly enhance my features.

I looked in the mirror and liked what I saw—no, I *loved* what I saw. Each day in this profession made it easier and easier for me to be proud of myself, proud of my looks and most importantly, proud of my accomplishments. Right now, I welcomed New York's nightlife as a much-needed break from those accomplishments.

Princess' boyfriend and his friend, who happened to be a teammate, showed up close to nine o'clock that evening. When Princess opened the door, I took one step backward, stunned. *My Lord, they are huge!* I said to myself. I'd never seen a professional football player in person in a stadium, let alone in a small room. I hoped they didn't notice me staring them up and down. And heaven forbid, I hoped my mouth wasn't hanging open as I gave them the once over.

Princess ushered them into the room. As they each extended their hands in an introductory fashion, Princess grabbed her date, smiled devilishly and said, "This one's mine." She referred to the larger of the two. *Good!* I thought. *I wouldn't know what to do with that much man.*

Our first stop of the evening landed us at one of the hottest clubs in New York City. The line of people waiting to get in, which wrapped all the way around the corner, indicated as much.

"Wait here," Princess' big guy said as he strolled confidently and coolly over to the bouncer. Within minutes, we were escorted to the front of the line, then straight up to the VIP level inside. How impressive! It was just like the movies! It reminded me of stories I'd heard of the infamous Studio 54: if you were somebody, you got in; if you weren't, you didn't. Period.

Once my eyes adjusted to the darkness inside, I could not believe what I saw. The walls pulsed with music—heavy on the bass; the DJ spun tunes on a raised platform; barely dressed dancers moved provocatively to the music on elevated risers, strategically placed throughout the room. Folks were gyrating, grinding and sweating on every inch of the dance floor.

We eventually made our way to a booth overlooking the incredibly large dance floor and slid into it. The guys asked what we wanted to drink.

"Sprite," I answered. My date gave me an "Are you crazy?" look, then a pleasant smile. I didn't drink alcohol, so what was I supposed to say?

We talked for a while, then headed to the dance floor. I love to dance, so I could hardly wait for this part. We partied all night, jumping from club to club, receiving the same VIP treatment all over the city. Being treated like royalty at the clubs felt good. It was so exciting!

As the night wore on, I watched couples everywhere, hanging all over each other. They were kissing and groping on the dance floor and at their tables. I grew more and more uncomfortable. My date got a little too close for comfort a couple of times; but I shied away and he got the hint. I didn't want to lead him on and certainly didn't feel obligated to give up anything.

The more I watched, the worse I felt. The night was becoming un-fun. I felt an underlying pressure to make a decision concerning the direction our "party" was heading. I politely excused myself and caught a cab back to the hotel. Of course, the next day when discussing the previous night's events, Princess felt I read too much into the whole situation and reiterated that no one would pressure me into anything.

That little taste of celebrity life came equipped with some very good moments, but I also learned a big lesson in the process: one must always stay in control of the situation, whether in a business deal or on a date with a handsome professional football player. The way to stay in control is through mental preparation. Know your limitations and prepare your mind ahead of time to stay within those boundaries.

For some reason, that night I envisioned myself getting in over my head; so I chose to stop matters before they even got started. I eventually did the right thing according to my moral standards; however, I made a promise to myself that next time, I would be more emotionally prepared from the beginning.

BE-You-TIFUL
TRINITY

Decisions, Decisions!
PRACTICAL APPLICATION

Growing up, I often heard older people in the church say "new levels, new devils." I didn't really know what that meant until later in life. They were saying that, as you're promoted in life, you'll be faced with new demons—new problems, new stresses, new temptations—and with making decisions about them.

When I joined the *Ebony Fashion Fair* crew in 1999, I had never really been faced with the party life, men and sex. Once I was, I had to make life decisions about those things.

The expression of God's love is evident in not only His infinite creation, but even more so in His gift of free will—the freedom to choose. Once we recognize this, it becomes our responsibility to use this God-given right wisely, not abuse it.

The key to making good choices is not in our ability to divine what's right and wrong—that's already built into our consciousness. The key to making correct choices lies in our *listening skills.*

Our listening skills provide us with *choices.* The Apostle Paul wrote, "Faith comes from hearing the message..." (Romans 10:17) and what we *hear* we process and commit to through *action.* The second half of Paul's sentence is the key to making right decision: "...and the message is heard through the word of Christ."

Be-You-Tiful Decision-Making Trinity

We succeed by making good decisions. Here are three ideas I think lead to Be-You-Tiful decisions:

1. Make choices based on what *you* believe.

A choice is generated from belief in something—a person, an idea, a fact. You can't unmake a choice once it's made, but your sincerity and selflessness in making choices and your effort to base your choices on true facts may allow you to weather bad ones.

We all believe differently and have our own perceptions of life, but there is only one way of thinking that will guarantee success— God's way of thinking. One true standard for knowing how God thinks is Jesus Christ. In revealing the nature of God to us, He serves as our example for making the right decisions.

2. Make choices based on knowledge.

The mind is built to import, process and act on information, but it is impossible to make a good decision from bad data. Decisions are made every day from unguarded, unhealthy, uneducated, misguided and manipulated mindsets.

A careless thought can be as dangerous as carrying out a bad decision, so we must be alert to the information we allow to touch our spirits. We can't afford not to manage our thoughts, no matter how tedious and inconvenient it may seem. Keep in mind that your choices affect not only you, but others, so pay attention to the information available to you and use it to build the right mindset.

3. Make choices based on the right motive and intent.

A bad choice is sometimes the result of ignorance—which can easily be caused by lazy thinking or a lack of knowledge—but we also make choices out of selfish desire. When this happens, it's impossible for our choices to bear good fruit.

Christ talks about this in the Gospel of Matthew. He says clearly that a good tree will not produce bad fruit nor a bad tree good fruit. A wrong motive will ultimately produce bad results; only right motives have a hope of producing good ones. Whatever decisions you make— and you'll make millions of them in life—you will reap the consequences, so make sure your intentions are pure and your heart is right before you make important decisions.

CHAPTER NINE

Poised

NEXT TIME CAME SOONER THAN I EXPECTED when we traveled to Baltimore the following weekend. Now that was a city I absolutely fell in love with! From its multi-cultural neighborhoods, dignified Victorian row houses with their historical architecture, graceful parks and gigantic outdoor food market, to its impressive downtown skyline against Inner Harbor, Baltimore offered so much.

After our show, the members of the charitable organization hosting the show in Baltimore escorted us back to the beautiful Hyatt Regency Hotel overlooking the waterfront. In their second-floor atrium, they staged a huge party for the models and special guests. We signed autographs, mingled with the gawking crowds and stuffed our faces with some good ole' Chesapeake Bay seafood.

That particular day, I felt on top of the world. I just don't know what my father saw all those years when telling me I was "ugly like my momma," because at least a hundred thousand times since becoming an *Ebony Fashion Fair* model, I had been told I was absolutely beautiful. I decided to trade in the negative images for the positive ones.

I smiled until my face seemed frozen that way; I shook hands and signed autographs until my hands were numb. Then I snuck off to the lobby with a plate full of food; I just wanted to be alone. I found a seat far enough away from the crush of people for solitude but still within eyesight of the festivities. Carefully balancing my plate on my knees, I chowed down on the most delectable jumbo gulf shrimp, crab cakes and stuffed mushrooms I'd ever tasted.

As a fork-full of crabmeat neared my mouth, a smooth, deep voice from behind startled me. "You must be hungry." The sudden words nearly caused my fork to veer off course.

I turned quickly to observe a tall, grinning young man with coconut brown skin clad in a very expensive suit. I'd trained my eyes to distinguish designers' styles. He was well built with a strong sense of self-confidence...or was that arrogance?

I nodded at him, then turned back to steer that fork to its destination. Just then, an obnoxious, shrill greeting from across the lobby startled me again. Princess. Would I ever get to finish my food in peace? I hadn't eaten all day and I had only one goal at that moment: to finish this delicious plate of food.

Princess charged the well-dressed, young man and they hugged, unlocked bodies, looked each other up and down, then hugged again as if they hadn't seen each other in years. I examined him a little more intently and his face looked familiar. I couldn't place his name, so I resumed eating, figuring introductions would come soon enough.

Princess eventually turned to me and introduced him as her childhood friend, Mark—another NFL player. I recognized him as a key player from the Seattle Seahawks the minute he told me his full name. In fact, the only reason his face looked familiar was because of a sports news story I just happened to see, declaring him to be on the "disabled list" due to an injury. They continued chatting—Princess much more than Mark—as they strolled toward the crowded ballroom.

A few moments later, as I arose to return my very empty plate to the bus table, Princess returned with a bubbly rendition of her chance meeting with Mark. As I correctly deduced, they hadn't seen each other in years. She also reported that he had been watching me since arriving and wanted to get to know me better.

"Are you interested?" she asked doubtfully, anticipating a negative response.

I shook my head with a kind smile, "No."

"I didn't think so," she said, shrugging. "That's cool."

It wasn't so much lack of interest as it was inexperience, but I couldn't share with anyone—not even Princess—the fact that I wouldn't know what to do with a man even if I had one. A part of me still feared men; a greater part than I knew, I realized. How strange...I liked the attention I got from men, but that was about it. Anything beyond that terrified me.

Princess must have shared the news with Mark because within

moments, I watched him shift his "pick-up" efforts to one of the other models, Micah. *Bingo!* He succeeded. I enjoyed watching the interaction. I needed to learn. And boy, did I have a lot to learn.

🎭

The following Monday, our show traveled to Silver Springs, Maryland. Mark, who remained in town visiting a friend, attended the show, then waited for us afterward. He invited Princess and I out to dinner, along with Micah, his new "main squeeze." Princess, Micah and I slid onto the custom leather seats of his beautiful, shiny black Escalade and headed to Baltimore to meet up with a few of his buddies from the Baltimore Ravens team for Jada's Lesson Number Two in Partying 101.

I absolutely enjoyed the novelty of all that public attention. We arrived at an exquisitely styled restaurant—I didn't even bother to look at the name. The bright lights and all of the fussing over us must have paralyzed my mind. Mark frequented that restaurant during the season and had come to know the owner, managers and chef quite well. It amazed me to see how money and a big name motivated the hostesses and wait staff to ensure that we had an extraordinary dining experience at their establishment. I tried to imagine how those same people would treat "ordinary" folks.

The waiter offered selections of wines to taste. The bottle Mark chose cost *six hundred dollars*. The price floored me! Even though I would not be drinking any to find out, I wondered how much better a six hundred dollar bottle of wine could taste than a one hundred or even fifty dollar one. I gave Princess a reserved, "I can't believe this" look.

She winked, then leaned over to me, whispering, "This is how we roll. Get used to it."

A few minutes later, we noticed that some of the wait staff had scurried toward the front, while one rushed quickly to the back, emerging with his manager. Others perched next to the bar along with the bartender, all waiting patiently for something. I couldn't imagine what, but soon found out.

Two huge six-feet-plus, brown-skinned Baltimore Ravens players—the smaller of the two, Ron, a Most Valuable Player hopeful—promenaded through the doors; and it seemed as if the entire restaurant came to a halt. The hostesses and manager grinned and greeted them, ushered them in from the foyer and escorted them to their seats. They did everything but bow and kiss their feet. If any other patron needed something in that moment, it'd just have to wait. After all, being one of the top defenders in the entire NFL, not to mention being in line for League MVP, automatically ranks you right up there with the President of the United States when it comes to public and media attention.

The players smiled and nodded at the staff and patrons before reaching our table and taking their seats next to Mark. Folks continued staring our way, some even venturing over for autographs.

You have to understand that at that time, Baltimore was looking forward to their first trip to the Super Bowl. Most of that hope hinged on the new coach and the magic Ron performed on the field. So everywhere Ron went, the spotlight followed.

You sort of learn to just "keep doing" in spite of the spotlight. That evening, we just kept enjoying our meal and each other's company. Mark suggested what to order and the food truly represented the chef's best. I had never tasted a steak so good and could not imagine one prepared any better. With the wine costing what it did, I could only imagine how much that steak cost. I had already learned—although I can't remember from where, perhaps from watching movies—that in fancy restaurants like that, prices aren't listed and you just don't ask. After all, you know what they say: if you have to ask, then you probably can't afford it.

Ron kept the whole table entertained and laughing with his comical, down-to-earth humor. He intrigued me. That restaurant outing was the most fun I'd had since leaving Chicago for our nine-month tour, in spite of the occasional intrusion of adoring patrons. I can't really call it an intrusion, though. As I stated earlier, I draw my energy from the audience while on stage and I guess it's no different when there is an audience *off* stage.

Later, when Princess, Micah and I walked to the ladies room, it was just like walking down the runway. We were learning: in spite of the spotlight, just keep going—just keep doing.

Even though six shows a week meant a super hectic and stressful schedule, we certainly made up for it by "getting our groove on" during that one day off. We looked forward to the weekends where we were usually in cities such as New York, Baltimore, Boston, DC and next on our tour, Buffalo.

In just about every major city we performed, entertainment by the professional athletes of that city came as part of the deal—a "sports package," I guess you could say. They loved beautiful women, and we loved having a good time. Or, at least, I was learning to love having a good time; learning to enjoy being in the spotlight.

November 1999—as we bid farewell to our last stop, Charlotte, with all its Southern flair and grandeur, we anxiously headed back home to Chicago. There, at the Arie Crown Theater—which houses one of Chicago's largest stages—we hosted one of our biggest shows of the year.

With those first three months on the road reduced to a blur for most of the crew, thoughts of going home for a short Thanksgiving break took precedence over walking down a runway. But for us swimsuit models, there was the added nervousness of the looming preview of the swimsuit layout that was about to appear in *Ebony*.

The photographer had shot the photos for the layout three months earlier—actually, the day after our tour started. So on that long-awaited day, we sat in a room of the Johnson Publishing building on the edge of our seats until the photos were finally brought in.

Was that really me in that swimsuit? It amazed me what the experts could do to a model's photo to make her look fantastic. Even though I looked pretty good to my outer eyes, my inner eyes began spotting all kinds of flaws. Through God's grace and Mom's guidance, I gained the ability to quickly shut tight those inner eyes—the windows to those old, haunting negative thoughts—whenever they tried to open.

While viewing the photos, my mind flashed back to the day of the shoot; the day Princess, Katrice, Candace and I had skillfully and tirelessly given our all for that swimsuit layout—tucking our abs in as far as they would go. That day, Mrs. Johnson's assistant had come into the studio with a white sheet of paper in his hand and whisked me out to the hallway.

"Jada, wait here while I go get Mrs. Johnson."

He left me standing in the main lobby of the Johnson building in a skimpy little two-piece swimsuit, with employees staring and smiling as they passed by. The lobby guard certainly got his eyeful that day. If I were on stage, I could stand there with confidence, but something about standing in an office lobby half-naked was quite unsettling. Even more unsettling was the fact I couldn't begin to imagine what Mrs. Johnson wanted to talk to me about. I am sure it only took them three minutes or so to come for me, but it certainly seemed more like ten.

Mrs. Johnson shook my hand, then got right to the point. "Jada, I want to know if you would like to be our Assistant Commentator."

Although my insides trembled, I assertively answered, "Of course! What would I have to do?"

She nodded to her assistant to hand me the piece of paper he had been holding and asked me to read it. That seemed a simple enough task, especially since my past opportunities to speak in front of people prepared me for this. I read with as much personality and poise as I could muster up, then handed the paper back.

"Oh, that was wonderful. Just wonderful," Mrs. Johnson commended me.

I already felt pretty good about myself, but her compliment made me feel as though I had just read with the literary style and fluency of Maya Angelou.

"Okay, you've got the job," she beamed. "You are our new Assistant Commentator."

Add another exclamation point to my life!

BE-You-TIFUL
TRINITY

We Are What We Think
PRACTICAL APPLICATION

I have heard this truism many times: *you are what you think*. From it I have learned the very valuable lesson that my thoughts control my life. When I came to this revelation, I realized that I had the power to make changes in my life *from within*.

The Bible says clearly: "…whatever is true, whatever is noble, whatever is right, whatever is pure, whatever is lovely, whatever is admirable—if anything is excellent or praiseworthy—think about such things." (Philippians 4:8)

I understand why. Negative thoughts breed negativity in our lives. Positive thinking will positively enhance our lives. It seems like a no-brainer, doesn't it?

I started to practice the method of positive thinking in my everyday life. It wasn't easy, but I realized that I had to challenge myself to do something that was completely out-of-the-ordinary for me. It wasn't about the negative experiences that had knocked me down. It was about how I *viewed* those experiences and how wisdom encouraged me to get back up.

For example: When I was asked to audition for the Assistant Commentator position, the first thought that ran through my mind was, *Why me? There are so many other talented and more beautiful girls than me.* I couldn't believe someone actually thought I could hold such a position, even though I'd trained in public speaking.

I am forever amazed by how our thoughts can erect oversized monuments to Pain and Fear. A monument should serve as a memorial of positive accomplishments or victories, not of imagined failures or loss.

Be-You-Tiful Thoughts Trinity

Think of your purpose being bigger than your life or your existence.
Think of your talents and abilities as gifts for others.
Think of validating someone else, and in return you'll be exalted.

Put More Thought Into It

Maybe you believe your life is useless or you *think* you don't really have what it takes to be what you should be. Stop negativity at your ears and don't let it into your head. Drive it out by putting more thought into your future.

Think ahead: "I'm a great success!" You can only discover your talents and gifts by personalizing them and putting more thought into them.

Let's take inventory. Answer the questions below as honestly as you can.

A. What are your gifts and talents?

_____

_____

_____

B. What can you see yourself accomplishing with these abilities?

_____

_____

_____

C. Do you see yourself making a difference with what God has given you?

Yes / No

If not, why not?

_____

_____

_____

_____

If so, what difference can you make?

_____

_____

_____

_____

CHAPTER TEN

Distractions

WITH SO MANY POSITIVE THINGS going on in my life at that moment, there really wasn't much room left for the negative things of the past to pop up—that is, except for that one demon named "Fear." Fear always found time to haunt me, but I never realized how much until the first three-and-a-half months of that initial tour. Countless opportunities came for me to be with a man during that time. My feelings toward all those men stretched well beyond mere disinterest; I was terrified of them!

I feared rejection, desertion, mental or physical abuse and sex. I feared starting a relationship, and I feared having to end one that wasn't working. I feared lack of respect on the man's part or on mine. I feared lack of love from him or from me. You name it; if it related to men, I feared it.

I did not need a psychiatrist to tell me that the number one reason for this was my relationship with my father—or I should say the lack thereof. However, other influential male figures during my childhood years contributed to that dysfunction as well. It seemed that there were three negative behaviors which were consistent: abuse, sex without love and infidelity.

Abuse. I did not have to search too far beyond my own household to find other men just as abusive as my father. I remember numerous times watching one of my uncles beat on his wife. And how could I forget my male cousins who punched and hit me? Even though my return blows proved I was physically tough enough to take it, mentally I was anything but tough.

I remember the terrible, desperate thoughts of revenge that entered my young mind as a result of watching my father slap Momma around. I remember the thread of sanity that I clung to day after day, living the life of a reject. No one emerges unscathed from an abusive environment. Fear of the abuse being repeated in future relationships stifles a person's growth into a whole and trusting partner. And that failure to grow leaves them susceptible to the very same pattern of dysfunction they're trying to avoid.

Sex without love. I'd always believed that most men sought just one thing from a woman: sex. I found myself judging most men before I had a chance to get to know them. I assumed I knew what they wanted from me—the same thing that family friend with his "adult" games had wanted. His ignorance kept him from actually achieving his goal, but the men I was meeting now weren't ignorant.

Sex was designed to be a wonderful display of love between a man and a woman brought together through marriage vows—a joining of souls and lives. Therefore, in my mind, love was a prerequisite to sex. Devoid of love, sex takes on a wicked persona with the potential to confuse, deceive, destroy and abuse.

This is how I see it: men possess a knack for separating love and sex. They can go after sex without a single thought of love and commitment. Now I realize there are many women who choose sex without love as well, but I think most women psyche themselves into thinking love is part of the equation so they can justify their sexual activity.

As a young girl, I longed more than anything to feel loved. I also desired to feel wanted, cared for, needed and of course, secured. It came naturally for my mother to meet those needs. In her own special way—which didn't include much outward expression—she loved me, wanted me around, cared for my basic needs and needed me to help her feel complete. Ironically, even during times when things were at their worst financially for my family, I was at last able to enjoy a sense of security with my mother.

As for my father, fulfilling any of those needs was too tall an order. He didn't know—or didn't care—that a dad plays a *huge* role in laying a solid foundation for his daughter's future relationships with men. When I feared things, my father should have embraced me, laying a foundation for security in my life. When I lacked self-esteem, he should have encouraged me, laying a foundation for confidence in my life. Such a good foundation makes it easy to distinguish a loving relationship from a loveless relationship. Without it, how's a girl supposed to know one from the other?

Infidelity. That behavior of distrust and deceit remained my biggest fear about men, mainly because it seemed so hard to see it coming and so hard to recover from it when it did. After watching my father cheat on my mother, I vowed to never let a man do that to me…as if I would have the ability to stop it. *Did I,* I asked myself, *have the ability to pick the right man to avoid that route altogether?*

My strategy to combat these types of relationship "issues" was to avoid relationships all together. I began to realize that as I got older, and as more men came across my path, that strategy was not likely to work.

✥

On February 14, 2000, at the close of our Valentine's Day show in Atlanta, Princess and I returned to our hotel room to be greeted by a huge bouquet of red roses. *Wow, how romantic!* I thought. *Just like in the movies.* Some man out there sure knew the way to a girl's heart. We both squealed with excitement as Princess pounced across her bed to reach the table where the roses sat.

"Who're they from? Who're they from?" I rushed her along. "I bet they're from your boyfriend!"

She grabbed the little white envelope propped in front of the vase by the hotel concierge and read it silently. "They're for you," she said.

Shocked, I began taxing my brain for possible suitors. *Who would be sending me flowers? Who even knew where I was?* It was flattering but perplexing. I opened the card and read it to myself.

The mystery began. It was an unsigned, short poem of admiration. I had a secret admirer. How cool!

Princess snatched the card back and read it again. "Ricky! I think Ricky's your secret admirer!"

Ricky, one of the models on tour with us, looked just like Shemar Moore, the young, dashingly handsome rising star of daytime TV soap operas. Come to think of it, Ricky did call me quite a bit…out of friendship, he said. So I'd never thought of us in any other way.

"Naw, it couldn't be Ricky," I concluded as I placed the vase on the table next to my bed. Thoughts raced through my mind of who my secret suitor could be. Princess shrugged her shoulders as she slipped out of her clothes and headed for the shower.

I called Mom to share the news of my roses. As I dialed Mom's number, I made a mental note to call my mother later as well. My mother and I did keep in touch on a somewhat regular basis, but it had always been easier to talk to my godmother about the more intimate details of my life.

I told Mom about Princess' suspicion regarding the roses and she agreed that it must be someone right under my nose. We continued talking about many other things—my exciting day-to-day occurrences; Rece's new job back home; and who Mom saw at the grocery store that told her to tell me "Hi." While still on the phone, there came a knock at our door. I opened the door, with cell phone to my ear, and smiled at the "Shemar look-a-like" standing there.

"Are you going out with the group?" he whispered. I shook my head "no." With that, he motioned—with his thumb and pinky finger next to his face—that he would call me later.

As I nodded and closed the door, my heart fluttered. Could that fluttering be an indication that I really did have some "more than friendly" feelings for Ricky? I'd certainly never thought about it before, but it caught my attention now.

A few minutes later, I hung up with Mom, then watched Princess fasten on her bracelet and grab a bottled water from the mini-fridge before we exchanged quick good-byes. While dashing out the door to catch up with the party-bound group, she paused, winked her eye and said, "Ricky" in a singsong tone.

I laughed and shook my head. I had grown to love being around Princess, but was glad to have the room to myself at that moment. My plans for the night included an HBO movie and my second favorite pig-out food: pizza (Krispy Kreme doughnuts being number one). I ordered the pizza, then prepared a steamy, hot bath, anxious to get on with my quiet, relaxing night.

Shortly after my pizza arrived and just as I settled nicely into a "tear-jerker" movie, a loud crash and bump came from the room next door. I quickly muted the TV volume so that I could interpret the commotion. A louder bump came, accompanied by yelling and cursing. I knew it was one of the models' rooms, but I could not remember whose. Both male and female voices projected at the top of their lungs as I jumped off my bed and ran, pajama-clad, into the hallway.

I raised my fist to pound on the door, remembering that Candace and Shantease shared that room. At that precise moment, the door flung open and Daryl, Candace's NFL-bound, college football player boyfriend, prepared to exit, but stood holding the door open while yelling some final irate words at her.

I busted in past him and stood in the middle of the war-zone looking room. Blankets strewn about the floor and a broken lamp smashed across the desk—it was a complete mess! With flashbacks of my mother and father in my childhood living room, I immediately went into aggressive Mediator mode, shouting, "What's going on here?"

Daryl, with fire in his eyes, shook a small book in his hand before hurling it at Candace, narrowly missing her face. He shouted a couple adjectives about her, saying in so many words that she was no good.

"You shouldn't have read my diary," Candace snapped, and the scene started making sense to me. I could only imagine what steamy information he'd read from those pages.

Daryl stormed out the room and down the hall. I took Candace back to my room and we ate pizza and talked.

"What did he read?" I questioned, already suspecting the answer but wanting to hear it straight from her mouth.

"Remember when I took that trip from Montgomery?" she asked, starting to tear up all over again.

Yes, I remembered it all too well. Candace had invited me to her room several weeks ago, wanting to discuss something. She'd looked very distraught.

"What's wrong?" I'd probed that morning.

"Would you pray for me?" she pleaded.

"Sure, but what's wrong?"

Tears had streamed down her cheeks as she explained a decision she was about to make; one that deep in her heart she knew was wrong. Therefore, she didn't feel very good about it.

"So don't do it," I said matter-of-factly. If it feels wrong, don't do it—this is not rocket science.

"It's not that simple," Candace insisted. She had recently met an NBA star who'd shown a lot of interest in her. He bought her a plane ticket to go and visit him for a day. Even though she had been dating Daryl for quite some time, she really felt something special with that new guy after their very brief encounter, so special she felt it warranted further exploration.

Her packed bags were already sitting by her door and her flight would leave that evening, just a few hours after our show finished. In her mind, it was a done deal. *So why pray about it now?* I remembered thinking to myself. But in order to console her, I prayed.

I never learned all the details about her trip, but I assume Daryl did when he read her diary. After that knock-down-drag-out incident, we never saw Daryl again. However, we were quite amused to find Candace suing him for unpaid debts on the Judge Judy TV show that following summer. Postscript: he never made it to the NFL.

I didn't know it at the time, but many of the painful experiences in my life prepared me to be there for some of the other models. It was funny how they would come to me for prayer or advice. I had learned so much about pain, fear, insecurity and making decisions that I felt like a counselor most of the time. I also learned that even though those models were beautiful on the outside, they had serious issues on the inside, just like me.

Valentine's Day 2000 in Atlanta marked the close of Candace and Daryl's chapter. At that same time, it was the beginning of a chapter entitled "Jada and Ricky."

※

Ricky called me as soon as he got in that night; just as he said he would. We talked on the phone for about forty-five minutes before I found myself standing at his door in my pink pajamas and matching slippers. He looked genuinely happy to see me, which made me feel so good. Every man should learn what it takes to make a woman feel special—like sending roses.

From the moment I arrived at his room, it was understood that I would be there for the night. Looking back, I guess going to his room in my pajamas was a sign of where the night was headed. Ricky and I talked and talked and talked. In between talking, we kissed and caressed. Nothing else.

Very soon, we became "an item." The two male models on our tour did not have roommates, which made it easy for our late-night rendezvous in Ricky's room to become a habit. In fact, from that date until our tour finished in May, I spent every night in his room.

At that time, sex was not the focal point of our relationship, which turned me on even more about Ricky. I confided in him about my inexperience with men and he offered to take matters as slow as I needed them to go. He did not antagonize me. He did not force me. He never even asked when I thought I would be ready. I loved that. It only took another month for me to get up enough courage to go to the next level.

Even though my mother and I never really talked much, she did encourage me to go to church. At church, I learned how important it was to save myself for my husband. Up until that point in my life, I was able to accomplish this. I was able to keep myself through junior high when most of my girlfriends were experimenting with sex. I was able to keep myself when many of my high school friends were deeply involved with their long-term courtships. I was even determined to refrain from sexual intercourse through college.

All of those years of abstinence and in one month I gave it all up. What was I thinking? How could I give in to temptation after all that? What made Ricky different from all of the other guys I'd been tempted by through the years? I believe the desperation and desire to be validated simply overwhelmed my moral consciousness.

Whatever my "reason," my decision to have sex with Ricky would forever change our relationship. Looking back I can now say, "I should have waited."

✦

That began a new era of understanding for me. *Was* I in love? Well, I was at least in love with the thought of being in love, and regardless of whether I was in love or not, the big question remained: Was *he* in love with *me*? The irony was that I had just become one of those women I mentioned earlier who psyched themselves into thinking love was somewhere in the equation just so that I could justify my sexual activity.

Sure I wanted a man to hold me and tell me he loved me, but only if he meant it. Ricky had never said those words; nor did I hold my breath in anticipation of hearing them. Of course I would much rather be sharing that type of intimacy with a man who had not only vowed to love me, but also vowed to be with me faithfully 'til death do us part. But Ricky was not up for that role. I wanted him to be, but my wanting him to be wasn't going to make it so.

With this new element in our relationship, Ricky and I stopped talking about our dreams and ambitions. Maybe we'd run out of things to talk about or maybe we simply left ourselves no time to talk. Either way, it made the relationship one-dimensional as the physical part upstaged the emotional and intellectual parts.

All those past apprehensions that had kept me free and clear of men in the first place surfaced again. But this time, I overcame them and put them in their place. I was going forward with this relationship!

After all, being in love with the thought of being in love had to count for something in making a relationship work, didn't it?

BE-You-TIFUL
TRINITY

Distractions, Distractions!
PRACTICAL APPLICATION

I have learned that distractions come in many different forms. Once I became aware of my weaknesses, I learned how to recognize and avoid many distractions. My Number One Distraction was men. Well, not *men* themselves, but the burning desire to be loved by them. The root of the weakness was the fear of not being loved and wanted.

There are no secrets when it comes to distractions. If we're sensitive to our spiritual reality, we can easily spot them. Where we get tripped up is when we willingly follow after our lustful desires instead. Take me, for example: instead of focusing on my career and spiritual calling, I found myself spending most of my time trying to make sure my boyfriend loved me and no one else.

The Master of Distractions (*Our Enemy*)

Instinctively, I think, we each know our purpose and what we need to achieve God's will for our lives. The Enemy within—the master of distractions—will not let up until he accomplishes his goal.

Here's a trio of distractions that Fear may put in your path. These distractions can:

1. **Change your course.**
    Picture yourself driving along the highway. You notice a roadblock

up ahead. There are detour signs put up to redirect the traffic. Your first instinct is to follow one of those other routes so you can continue your travel in the same direction, but the Enemy sets up roadblocks in such a way that it can cause you to focus on the roadblock itself. This draws your attention away from the road God had you on initially.

The roadblocks in life can make us impatient and prevent us from recognizing the detour signs that God provides to help us reach our intended destination.

2. Drain your resources.

Our job, family, talents and abilities are all resources given to us for a purpose. That purpose is to expand God's Kingdom. The Enemy is a master at taking your natural desire to see God's plan unfold and twisting it into impatience. Perhaps this comes in the form of a job that pays good money but that is really a distraction. Your focus shifts toward security and away from your true commitments in life.

This lack of focus can drain us emotionally by causing us to neglect our relationships in favor of pursuing money instead of the will of God. Yes, God wants us to have the good things of the Earth, but there is an ultimate plan even for those resources.

3. Make you change your commitment.

This is the deadliest distraction because the Enemy encourages you to become self-centered, to look to yourself for answers, to forget that you need God's help. If you can't save yourself, then how can you heal yourself, love yourself or feel good about yourself without God's help? Worst of all, thrown back on your own resources, you may try to develop your own solution for how to deal with economic, emotional and physical issues of life rather than accepting God's solution.

Exercise in Purpose

In discovering your true purpose in life, pay careful attention to distractions. In the space provided below, answer these two questions:

1. What is your purpose in life?
2. What are the distractions that keep you from fulfilling it?

My Purpose: _____

_____

_____

Distractions: _____

_____

_____

_____

CHAPTER ELEVEN

My Mic, My Passion

MY RELATIONSHIP WITH RICKY BECAME MY lifeline. I latched on to him with all the emotional strength I could muster. It was quite an easy feat thanks to my painful past—a haunting past that Ricky had no clue about. Somehow, in all those late night–and sometimes all-night–talks that we shared, my emotional scars didn't emerge as a topic.

Oh, I told him plenty about my father's suspected shenanigans with other women, drugs and drinking, and about how he'd deserted us in such a cruel and sneaky way. I told him about how my momma had to leave us with Ann Lee for a time until she could financially support us. I even told him about my penniless days when I lived with my godmother. But in all those illustrations of my strength and endurance in overcoming life's obstacles, Ricky could easily assume that those character-building opportunities did just that: build my character.

In all fairness to myself, my character had truly been built up as a result of the many trials I met and conquered. Unfortunately though, the emotional trauma from those events had built up as well. So, although Ricky must have noticed this emotional attachment, he perhaps had no clue as to why it was happening. It was easier for him to think it was due to his charms rather than my insecurities. Funny how emotions always seem to get lost in translation.

I drove myself nearly crazy in my quest to be perfect for him—to ensure that he would love me and never look in another woman's direction. The perfect bait for misery appeared, and I snatched it!

If only I had listened to Mom. She always said that I would only find true and unconditional love *inside* myself; because God is love, and God lives in all of us. It took me years to fully understand what she meant, simply because I tried to comprehend with my mind instead of my heart.

⚜

One day, I awoke totally frustrated by it all! Not only had I realized that "being in love with the thought of being loved" left me empty, but there were a few other things out of place in my life as well. For instance, I loved modeling, but it seemed modeling didn't love me back the way I needed it to. I couldn't deny the addicting energy of the runway that kept me yearning for more stage time, and I certainly couldn't deny the exhilarating high I encountered each time I put on a Bob Mackie, Anna Sui, Marc Bouwer or other designer masterpiece, but was that all there was? A resounding "NO!" came from my heart.

The missing link pointed back to broadcasting. Even though I relished following in the stiletto footsteps of Naomi and Tyra, I also desired to follow in the dynamic, journalistic footsteps of Oprah. Immediately, I began feeling an inner tickle of criticism about not finishing college. All my good intentions of going back to college after doing the conference tour with Mom were interrupted by modeling.

I iced those thoughts with a cool, *So what? All in all, it turned out to be a good interruption; no condemnation, please.*

I'd walked away from Contra Costa College armed with invaluable wisdom, mainly to the credit of my English teacher, Ms. Wander. She'd had the greatest impact on my broadcasting education. Entering Ms. Wander's class my first day, I sensed something very different about her. My suspicion was soon confirmed when she opened her mouth to speak. A short woman topped with gray hair, she projected a voice that rang the rafters due to her being deaf. She required the assistance of a sign interpreter. Watching them interact throughout the semester intrigued me; so much that my sister and I later enrolled in a sign language class.

I believe that communication is the highest privilege given to us by God. Whether its verbal, written, sign or perhaps even a glance into someone's eyes, its potential for effectiveness only intensifies when it passes between individuals. I guess that is why I am absolutely captivated by the art of communication.

Ms. Wander noticed that about me. Aside from her curriculum, she showed interest in me, believed in me, even told me I had an amazing presence. I'd left that college feeling positive about my talent and wanting to make Ms. Wander proud.

Where had that gone? Even Mom used to tell me all the time that I was destined to preach. But my desire to model had vastly overshadowed all thoughts of heeding the speaking call.

Until now.

My determination to be a talk show host began midway into that first tour. I thank God that I'd invested toward that goal years prior to becoming an *Ebony Fashion Fair* model. I'd taught myself a great deal of the basics of public speaking during those years of traveling with Mom—practicing for hours and hours. Sometimes I would record myself reading out loud so I could hear my voice with my outer ears, as others do. Other times, I would speak in front of the mirror, checking my delivery and stance.

So when Mrs. Johnson asked me to read for her in that lobby, my readiness was no coincidence. In fact, I do not believe in coincidence or luck when it comes to success. Instead, success occurs when God opens the right doors and opportunity meets preparedness. That same opportunity to read for Mrs. Johnson could have come my way when I was not prepared; had I fumbled through it, that assistant commentator position would not have been granted.

I didn't fumble. I was ready and willing to play the part and the part was mine: assistant commentator for the world's largest traveling fashion show! What an awesome title to put on a resume.

Up to that point—midway through our tour, when I woke up that morning exasperated—that's all it was, a title. As *assistant* commentator, I was never asked to take on any part of a commentating role in the show. But that didn't stop me from doing my own self-study of that role!

I very wisely observed the commentator on every possible occasion. My mind captured every word she spoke and every inflection in her voice as I strutted down the runway. Exiting the stage amidst roaring applause, I would catch a glimpse at her poise and self-assurance.

Models can strut all night long, but with no one describing their outfits—or worse yet, with a disorganized or ho-hum presenter—the show can flop. The opposite is true as well—a good commentator can "make" a show. As a result, models and commentators highly respect each others' roles.

During one of our stops in Alabama, opportunity for advancement once again came my way. Once again, I was prepared…well, almost.

As we arrived at the convention center a couple hours before that evening's show, Steve Williams, our stage manager, approached me with news that took me totally by surprise. Our commentator had had a death in her family and would be heading back home for a few days.

"When is she leaving?" I solemnly asked. In the back of my mind, I knew this meant they needed me to stand in, but a wave of sympathy hit me. What must she be going through? In the months I had come to know her, what I initially took for arrogance was really just high self-esteem. And that tough outer shell housed a very soft heart. I had come to admire her work ethic and her style.

"Tonight," he answered.

"Whoa." My mouth dropped open and my eyebrows shot up. Talk about short notice! Thoughts of me stepping into such a major role came into stunning focus.

Never would I have imagined that my introduction into the commentating world of *Ebony Fashion Fair* would be like this. Come to think of it, I never imagined at all how it would be. And now…well, the show had to go on. Fortunately for me, this occurred right before a two-day break of which I used every minute to get ready.

The main challenge in commentating a fashion show is learning the unique, precise descriptions of about two hundred garments. And because of all the action packed into a two-hour show, cues become extremely important for the models. The commentator must set the rhythm of the entire performance in order to deliver those cues flawlessly.

On show day, I arrived backstage a nervous wreck! There was so much to remember, so much riding on me to get it all right. How could I possibly pull this off? Someone told me the show was sold out. *Oh great,* I thought, *just what I need: an auditorium packed with hundreds of people staring at me.*

I took a moment to pray, thanking God for His protection throughout that show, just as He had already protected me through everything else
in my life. Then, with newfound confidence, I slipped on my very expensive, chocolate brown Marc Bouwer dress. Its open midriff and thigh-high
split were characteristic of the trend-setting designer whose clients include
Toni Braxton and Halle Berry. Heck, I *felt* like Toni every time I wore a
Marc Bouwer dress.

I looked stunning. As I looked over my shoulder into the mirror, I
chuckled at the notion that even if I didn't perform well, at least I looked
good. One last glance in the mirror and it was show time!

✼

That night, the microphone became my very best friend. All I'd learned
before about using a mic seemed to climax in that magical moment as I
captivated that crowd with my voice. The relationship between me and that
mic for one hundred and twenty minutes was fulfilling. In fact, I had
learned in broadcasting classes to become one with the microphone.

I held onto that mic with the most natural passion I'd ever experienced. My heart beat with pleasure beyond words. I gained strength
moment-by-moment knowing that it felt right because it *was* right. My
voice rolled softly and delicately across the mic when needed, then boldly
and playfully when the moment called for that—everything perfect, every
harmonic moment right on cue.

I loved the power of the mic. I loved being in control. What a daring
and exciting feeling to know that the success of the entire show hinged on
me and on my relationship with the mic. I was in love with that microphone, and it *did* love me back!

BE-You-TIFUL
TRINITY

Passion
PRACTICAL APPLICATION

There are moments in our lives when we experience true happiness. There were two particular moments in mine when I felt a real sense of joy and wholeness: when I gave my life to Jesus Christ and when I picked up the microphone for the very first time.

I felt a high level of satisfaction and fulfillment when I picked up that mic because I knew that, at that moment, I was right where God wanted me to be. We have to keep things in perspective; it wasn't just about me experiencing a new level of success in my career. More importantly, there was a covenant made—an *exchange* that took place when I chose to pursue my purpose over my fears.

How was I aware of the exchange? I felt an inner peace combined with an assurance that I was pursing my true passion and was in accord with God's perfect will.

I believe in this great replacement plan God offers us with all my heart, soul and mind. I decided to pursue God's will and take the exchange in pursuing my purpose over doubt in my abilities, hatred toward my dad and the fear of never being loved. True joy and happiness comes from our learning to choose the right things in life and not settling for less.

I'm not embarrassed or ashamed to share with people the struggles of my past because I'm fully aware of God's promises for my future. I used to wake up with bitterness, but now I wake up with gladness. I used to wake up feeling worthless, but now I wake up with confidence.

What I am saying to you is that through a *covenant* with Jesus Christ, each of us can exchange our struggles for blessings.

Take the Exchange

Our covenant with God empowers and entitles us to make wonderful exchanges in all three levels of existence: Spirit, Soul and Body.

1. Spirit
Exchange:
- Anger and hatred for love and kindness.
- Fear and doubt for trust and faithfulness.
- Disappointment and failure for thankfulness and victories.
- Pain and heartache for joy and peace.
- Ashes of guilt and shame for confidence, beauty and honor.
- Anxiety and frustration for patience and rest.
- Sinful nature for goodness and righteousness.

2. Soul
Exchange:
- Spiritual death for eternal life in heaven.
- Shallow material/physical life for true life through Jesus Christ.
- Danger and uncertainty for complete safety.
- Spiritual thirst and hunger for true satisfaction for your soul.

3. Body
Exchange:
- Poverty and lack of means for daily provision.
- Shattered dreams and broken promises for restoration and success.
- Sickness and pain for healing and good health.
- Loneliness for good friends and healthy relationships.
- Deprivation and abandonment for help and assistance.
- Dull career and financial struggle for knowledge that leads to wealth.
- Shallow affection and sexual hunger for real love, union and fulfillment.

CHAPTER TWELVE

Family

THEY SAY EVERYONE WILL GET ABOUT FIFTEEN MINUTES of fame. Some of us get more than that, whether for good or for ill, whether it's fair or not. In the final analysis, life's not about the minutes or hours or years of fame. And it's not about being in love with the thought of being in love. It's about family. My accomplishments pleased me, but they didn't matter—not really—unless my family was pleased with them.

To say they were pleased is an understatement. To this day, they collect every photograph or magazine that I have been in—simply amazed to see one of their own there. Even though my immediate family has shown nothing but genuine happiness for me, I have felt the doubtful eyes of others on me. I suppose they were trying to determine just how far this modeling thing would take me.

However, my drive to excel extends far beyond my family and friends as the whole African-American community has an opportunity to fix their eyes on me from time to time and pass judgment. As a representative of the world's most successful black-owned cosmetic company, not to mention a direct reflection on the world's largest traveling fashion show, living up to others' measurements of success has always been part of my career. It can be a tall order.

The public doesn't realize how much undue pressure is placed on celebrities to do right—on stage and off stage. Of course, in the fans' mind, their judgment is harmless, but when you multiply that one innocent, unrealistic expectation by millions, then it can become overwhelming for the celebrity. But fans are just doing what fans do best: expecting things. And I must always do what I do best: perform beyond their expectations.

In April of 2000, we traveled to my home state of California, performing in Los Angeles, Sacramento, the San Francisco Bay Area plus a handful of other cities in the surrounding areas. Just the thought of a trip back home conjured up a whirlwind of emotions. In the space of a moment, my excitement gave way to anxiousness; my confidence backpedaled to doubt; and my composure fluttered away into restlessness.

Going back home in this new capacity felt weird. It was sort of like having "made it," but still carrying my old baggage—and oh, what terrible memories, feelings, thoughts and attitudes were stuffed into that baggage!

I suppose those see-saw emotions had a lot to do with the fact that I had not been home in such a long time. *How will they respond to me?* I had not seen most of my family in years—least of all my father. My relationship with him was still strained, so I really didn't care what he thought about me or my career. Okay, so maybe I did care a little, but what daughter doesn't yearn for the approval of her Daddy?

Our West Coast tour began in Los Angeles instead of San Francisco, buying me more time to get my emotions in check before performing for my family. I was glad for that reason, of course, but mainly glad of the sheer thrill of being in the City of Angels.

To this day, we rank the L.A. show highly because of the fashion-consciousness of Hollywood. We just never know what designing mogul, supermodel or famous actor will be sitting in our audience. For instance, that first year, I had the pleasure of meeting Kenya Moore, former Miss USA and strikingly beautiful TV and film actress. We enjoyed an enlightening conversation during the after-party. I praised her for her amazing work, and shared my belief that she will do great things in the film industry.

Talking to Kenya brought to mind the ever-so-unfair, ever-so-real barriers to superstar status that so many talented black female Hollywood figures face—actresses, producers and directors alike. I continue to pray that all that changes in my lifetime.

After the flashiness of the shows in the L.A. area, Sacramento, with its millions of evergreens and fruit trees, provided a mellow safe haven for us. Princess and I dined with a couple of her basketball player friends from the Sacramento Kings. We talked and laughed over escargot and some of California's greatest wine from the nearby Sonoma vineyards (I still wasn't drinking). At that point, I began hungering for my hometown. The next day we would be there, but I longed to be there at that moment.

I guess I never gave much thought to being homesick for the San Francisco Bay Area since my family moved to Tennessee so long ago. Whether or not I was ever homesick in the past didn't matter; I was now and wanted tomorrow to come quickly.

Finally, my day of reckoning in San Francisco arrived. Oh, what a day! But first, let me share with you the most wonderful part of all.

I anxiously jumped off the bus before anyone else after it *crawled* to a stop at the Cathedral Hill Hotel. I stepped through the lobby doors and into the open arms of happy family members—including my mother, Rece and Mom. They'd flown in from Tennessee earlier that day and already checked into their rooms here at the same hotel. I knew they were as thrilled as I to be back in the Bay Area.

I guess I never realized until that moment just how much I missed my family. A sweet reunion; complete with tears of joy! Even when my mother and I hugged in that lobby, something felt miraculously different—as though the atmosphere gave way to a whole new declaration of acceptance. We had never experienced the typical mother-daughter relationship. In fact, from early childhood through today, my mother has been BJ to me. Not Mom, Mommy, Momma or Mother—just BJ, as everyone else called her. Only recently have I come to think of her as "Momma."

I think I understand what contributed to this distance between us: her young age at the time of my birth; an upbringing that made the usual barriers between family elders and kids a bit fuzzy; the fact that she didn't raise me during my entire childhood; and I think a certain lack of respect I felt for her during her lengthy, abusive era with my father. There was no make-or-break moment between us, no unforgivable act or watershed event. Just a weak and uncertain bond.

But in the moment I walked into that lobby, I sensed that my relationship with my mother was headed in a new direction. In her own non-sentimental way, her heart reached out to mine, desiring to mend rifts of the past. And in my emotionally distant way, my heart responded to hers with, *Don't worry about it—it's not your fault; things just happened the way they happened.*

In that hotel lobby, in the midst of all the hugs and tears, I caught a glimpse of Ricky walking by with the other models. He flashed me a cold look, then blew me a sarcastic kiss. I quickly glanced away, giving my attention to Rece and commenting on how great her hair looked.

Ricky and I had had a long talk prior to that San Francisco trip. I told him that I would not be introducing him to my family—not as a boyfriend, that is. I assured him that it had nothing to do with him personally, but that Mom would be totally against my involvement with *any* guy, since she felt at that point, all my attention needed to be focused on my career.

Was that really it? I asked myself. *Would I believe that if I were Ricky?*

Ricky was hurt and angry at the thought of not being properly acknowledged. He felt rejected and told me as much. I felt badly; he had a right to be angry. After all, we had been "an item" for over four months. Everyone on tour knew it. Then suddenly—it seemed to him—I was saying he wasn't a "good enough item" for my family. But when I looked at my feelings for Ricky, I honestly wasn't sure if we were a "real" item or not. We never talked about it. We hardly talked about anything any more. And frankly, the whole situation was a little bit humiliating to me—as far as I knew I was just another conquest for him. I really wasn't sure.

In spite of all this, I stood my ground, not swaying from my decision to keep our relationship a secret. It didn't occur to me that the fact that he was hurt by not being introduced to my family indicated how he felt about me—how was I supposed to know that?

In the depths of my heart, I knew that having sex with Ricky was wrong. The funny thing was I frantically tried to hide that immorality from Mom, forgetting—or perhaps not really understanding—that all along, *nothing* was hidden from God.

See, I didn't have a personal relationship with God then as I do today. So I just never considered His omnipresence and omnipotence. I suspect I'd have done a lot of things differently if I'd realized He was everywhere, knowing everything. For starters, I would have been talking to Him a lot about my problems instead of letting them boil down into hateful goo. But at that point, my only channel to Him was Mom. By fearing *her*, and fearing what *she* thought of my decisions, I subconsciously feared—or reverenced—God.

Eventually Ricky saw my point of view and conceded to remaining anonymous to my family. We agreed that I would tell them about him soon, but just not that trip. He was still highly offended, though, and it showed.

Mainly out of guilt toward Ricky, I decided to still show him as much attention as possible that entire weekend. What a foolish thing to do! I nearly wore myself out before and after the show, sneaking to Ricky's room in between visits to my own room and Mom's room.

⚜

All my family members and some friends who lived in the area attended our Saturday night San Francisco show. Nervousness came over me before that show like never before. I guess I felt the pressure of having to prove to all of them who Jada Jackson, the *Ebony Fashion Fair* model, was. That self-inflicted pressure lifted as soon as I heard the "oohs," "aahs" and cheers each time I pranced down the runway. I realized they would have loved me even if I'd fallen over my feet on that stage! I could do no wrong; I was their hero.

That night, I stepped into star status, validated by my family. Forget what the public or the press thought; my family and friends thought I was great and that was all that mattered. Their mere presence encouraged me, but to hear them proudly call my name blessed me immensely. I operated totally in my "zone" that night, doing what came naturally to me—only this time, there was a higher step to my strut; more glide to my stride and even sharper hip action to my pivot.

⚜

I couldn't believe my eyes, but after the show, there must have been about a hundred family members and friends gathered around me in the lobby! How awesome to realize just how many relatives I actually had supporting me. I introduced some of the models to as many family members as I could. The scene reminded me of when we'd performed in Princess' hometown of Cleveland and she'd introduced us to her crowd of family and friends.

They swarmed all over me, spewing compliments, introductions and questions:

"Oh, Jada, you've grown up to be so beautiful!"

"You were fabulous! Gir-r-rl, how'd ya learn to walk like that?"

"This here's your cousin, Lawrence, that you never met."

"Look at how pretty you are!"

"I'm so proud of you!"

"You know Cousin Betty has a daughter who's tall like you; you think she can be a model, too?"

They went on and on for almost an hour. The attention: surreal. The love: overwhelming. I smiled for almost a hundred pictures and signed more autographs than I ever recalled signing. (Hmmm…signing my name for my own family. Fame definitely causes people to act strangely.)

I don't mind admitting that I thoroughly enjoyed being put on a pedestal by them that day. I could not have planned things any better, except of course, for the part where *he* came in.

In that sea of people; through all that mayhem, one obnoxious voice, one over-powering presence emerged from the crowd. "This here's *my* daughter. Can't I get a picture with my own daughter? Everybody else gonna have to wait! I want a picture, and I waited long enough."

At that moment, I had taken a short reprieve from picture taking and stood talking to my maternal grandmother's sister, Aunt Helen. When I heard that familiar voice, I glanced over my shoulder just in time for that boisterous, loud, un-loving, absentee father of mine to grab my arm and begin dragging me to where he had been lurking. In order to draw as little attention as possible to this already embarrassing moment, I bit my tongue and went with him.

He wanted to introduce me to his girlfriend, who sat on a bench along a wall. I couldn't care less about meeting her. I didn't want *him* there, so you can imagine how I felt about her, though she was probably an okay person in her own right.

The girlfriend stood and extended her right hand toward me during the introduction, her left hand clutching the door prize she had won during the show. I just nodded and gave a half smile, seeing her hand, but pretending not to.

My father shoved his camera in his girlfriend's extended hand and barked an order at her to take a picture of him and his beautiful daughter. He grinned with pride for the picture, hugging me as though he had been hugging me all my life.

As a model, you learn to smile even when there's nothing to smile about. Standing there, taking a picture with my father required me to draw on that lesson. Every second with him felt like an hour and he could not have made it more clear that he felt he had contributed to my accomplishments.

As my anger threatened to boil over, my aunt approached and grabbed my arm. "Jada, there are some people who want to see you."

As she pulled me in the direction of those people, my father yanked my other arm and pulled me in the opposite direction. I was caught in a tug-of-war as words of accusation and criticism flew between them. I released my arms from both their grips and quickly darted back to my dressing room to gather my bags.

Back at the hotel, I really didn't care to see anyone. Fortunately, Princess stayed out with some other models. I undressed, removed my make-up and showered—still fuming the whole time. I didn't know how, or to whom, to properly vent my anger.

Why did I let that man get to me like that?

Because you have never forgiven him.

Where did that voice come from? It came from inside me, yet sounded so loud in my ears that I jerked around, halfway expecting to find a person standing there. Even though I'd never heard that voice before, I was ninety-nine percent sure it was God!

And why should I forgive him for all the terrible things he did to my mother, sister and I? And really, God—that is, if this is You talking—how can You possibly expect me to forgive him when he doesn't think he's done anything wrong? He doesn't want my forgiveness.

Hating him is wrong.

There I sat in my room, arguing with God! I had to get out of there. I hurriedly threw on my jogging suit and snuck down the hall to Ricky's room. He opened the door wide, with an equally wide smile on his face, having already identified me through the peephole. Seeing him brought immediate comfort to me—so much so, I even managed to smile.

"Hey sugar-butt," he said smacking me on my behind as I walked past him. "I was just getting ready for bed."

I turned and embraced him for as long and as hard as I could. Tears flowed down my cheeks and onto his bare chest.

"Whoa, what's the matter, darlin'?" Ricky inquired as he lifted my chin so that our eyes could meet.

"I don't want to talk about it right now. Just hold me." He took that as an invitation to make love.

Sex with Ricky had become my security blanket, my strange coping mechanism for whatever wrong occurred in my life. A temporary fix at best, but nevertheless, the only one I knew. No longer did I fear men;

instead, I feared being without them. Okay, so I feared being without *Ricky.* I had never been with any other man; therefore, I couldn't really say that sentiment extended to the whole gender.

I *could* truthfully say that having his warm body next to mine became rather addictive to me. Even at times when I didn't enjoy the lovemaking, I accepted it as the better option when compared with being alone with my emotional "stuff." That sounds pathetic and unfortunately, that same rationale works for millions of other confused women, unsuccessful in their quest for true love.

I had just gotten back to my room and sure enough, the message light flashed on the hotel phone. I listened to Mom's message which presumed I was out with the other models. She stated that she would just see me at breakfast. I smiled at her accuracy: I *was* out with one of the models.

I prepared a hot bubble bath. As I slid into the tub, I closed off the world.

※

After an early Sunday breakfast with Mom, my mother and other kin, the tour bus pulled out at nine o'clock, heading across the Bay Bridge for our one o'clock Oakland show that afternoon. Mom and the others would meet us in Oakland later, after visiting some favorite spots there in the city and even our old neighborhood across the Bay. My schedule didn't allow for me to sightsee around town with them, but the opulence of the city was enough, coupled with my breathtaking view of the streets of San Francisco from my hotel window. With time being of the essence, that had to satisfy my hunger for now.

Even though most of the models tried to recover some of their lost sleep after partying into the wee hours, I kept our forty-minute bus ride to Oakland quite lively. I pointed out famous landmarks like Coit Tower and the stretch pyramid of the Trans-America Building, as well as other fun facts about the city while our bus driver, Bruce, grinned at my tour guide performance. Bruce (who still faithfully drives for us today), as my good friend and guardian angel all rolled into one, understood the excitement in my heart—the excitement of being back where it all began for me.

But at one point during the ride, I certainly caught the attention of more than just Bruce when I announced that my mother's sister, Aunt Delores, who lived in Rodeo, had invited the entire *Ebony Fashion Fair* crew to her house for a good ole' home-cooked dinner! It was a delightful break from the hotel and restaurant food we were subjected to throughout the entire nine-month tour. (In fact, I promised myself not to step foot in a restaurant during our summer break.) To top that off, she arranged for limousines to transport us to and from her home! How generous of Aunt Delores—especially since I hadn't talked to her in years. But it actually didn't shock me that she would do something like that—she was the soul of generosity.

At the conclusion of our Oakland show—and just as my mother "BJ" informed me—two white, stretch limos awaited us to take us to the dinner party. There was much laughter and carrying on in those limos during that ten-mile ride to her home in one of Rodeo's well-established, upscale neighborhoods. The models and crewmembers alike all loved my relatives for their top-notch, Bay Area hospitality. In fact, Aunt Delores' home-cooked dinner party for the entire crew after the Oakland show has become an annual tradition.

That first annual dinner party at her house was truly awesome. All of my Grandma Ann Lee's brothers and sisters came to insure that my friends and I enjoyed ourselves. Along with Aunt Delores, my Uncle Elliott, Aunt Louise, Aunt Bobbie and Cousin Marsha—who always aspired to open a restaurant—helped prepare the food while Aunt Cecilia and a host of cousins contributed in a big way as well. My family must have hustled for days around that place, arranging the activities in such an impeccable fashion. We ate, and ate and ate—first the main course, then the most mouth-watering desserts. All the models kept my family well entertained with stories galore of famous people we'd met and backstage secrets we were privy to.

The day would have been complete if Grandma Ann Lee and Aunt Rachel were present. But Ann Lee had passed when I was seventeen. I still miss her. I remember that day as an eleven-year-old when she and I cried together after cussing each other out. That one time only, I got a quick glimpse of the real Ann Lee: a once-soft woman, hardened by life's cruelty.

Although Aunt Rachel was not around those days, her spirit lent itself to the occasion. Besides inspiring me toward modeling, she'd taught me to stand up to any man…which is exactly what I had to do that evening, thanks to my father.

Yes, indeed—he showed up for the party just as if he'd been invited and announced his presence loudly.

Why was he here anyway? I asked myself. None of the reasons I could think of at that moment were good. I'd made myself a success in spite of him and he had no right to be here. *At least*, I thought grimly, *he hadn't brought his half-his-age girlfriend along.*

"This here's *my* child!" he yelled, heading right to the table, stabbing at the leftovers. "When she was born, I named her Chanese. Ch-a-n-e-s-e. Chanese Marie Jackson. I don't call her no Jada. I named her; I named her." He kept pointing at his chest, apparently oblivious to the fact that he had a fork in his hand and would any minute stab his chin or something.

Yeah, so what? My real name was Chanese. I hated that name, which is why I changed it when I turned eighteen. I selected Jada Azaliah because in Hebrew it meant "Our God hath set aside." I looked up the meaning in a bible dictionary that was given to me by my momma. Although two separate words, I loved the meaning when they were put together. I had come to understand later in life that God really had set me aside for a special purpose on this earth.

I hated Chanese, and I did not like what my father was doing at that moment. Right then, Aunt Rachel's voice entered my head, *Don't take no crap.* I knew that man would not disappear by wishing him away. No, I had to open my mouth and do something.

Thankfully, much of what I said to my dad is a blur to this day, but I needed to demand respect from him—something that did not come easily. I had been so intimidated by the thought of his rejection, I found myself doing and saying things just so I wouldn't anger him. That's how desperate I was for him to love me. Not this time. This time I spoke my mind.

Out of respect for me, the crew members and models never mentioned the scene later, aside from a few stray questions about my real name and my real mother, whom they were shocked to learn was BJ. They just let it lie. But I couldn't. I had to demand respect. I was now an adult. I had to stop acting like a terrified little girl still hoping for others to change.

At that point, the truth of what Mom had told me for years became a reality. The only person I could change was myself. That became my quest.

BE-You-TIFUL
TRINITY

Taking Responsibility
PRACTICAL APPLICATION

Family—that's where my "family problems" began: fear, lack of confidence, insecurity and the list goes on. I believe that if we can survive our families, we can survive anything. Our families are where we learn how to co-exist in society and relationships. They are also a true test of our ability to do so. Unfortunately, most of our struggles, pain, abuse, emotional stress and financial burdens are cultivated right in our very own homes.

Even though we have difficulties and differences in our families, we must recognize that this God-given institution is the foundation of our religious communities and churches, our nations and the world. If the "priest" is inactive in the home, if there's no direction and no training in virtues taking place, how will a child learn virtue?

Our parents are commissioned by God to teach and demonstrate His love and also to establish fertile ground in which we can grow to become productive citizens and sound Christians. Yet children make the mistake of expecting parents to be perfect—which they never are. This internal conflict can quickly become ingrained in a child and produce the deadliest sins of all—judgment and the inability to forgive.

Responsibility is at the core of maturity. As we grow to adulthood, there comes a point at which we have to take responsibility for our part in our family's failures and successes.

Be-You-Tiful Responsibility

Do you care about the divine institution called the family? Do you want to contribute to the marvelous support system God has put in place for you or do you care more about your own survival?

Christ Jesus said: *"For whoever wants to save his life will lose it, but whoever loses his life for me will find it."* (Matthew 16:24-26)

Here is a trinity of Be-You-Tiful questions for you to consider about family life:

1. Responsibility: What role do you play in your family?
- Are you the one who stirs up drama and conflict or are you the one who mends the bridges and helps people forget about their differences? *Be a bridge-builder, not a pot-stirrer.*
- Are you a hindrance to someone else's growth? Are you enabling or disabling other family members who are trying to better themselves? *Be an enabler, not a disabler.*
- Are you the one who helps out whenever you're called upon or are you the one who can't be bothered? *Give back, don't give up.*

2. Communication: Who are you talking to in your family?
- Do you avoid certain family members because you don't care for them that much? *Remember the Golden Rule: "So in everything, do to others what you would have them do to you, for this sums up the Law and the Prophets."* (Matthew 7:12)
- Do you love to hear dirt on another family member? *Remember the Golden Rule!*
- Do you go out of your way to make sure that you welcome *everyone* or do you show partiality to particular family members? *Remember the Golden Rule!! And remember: God isn't partial, why should you be?*

3. Forgiveness: Have you forgiven your family? Have you asked for forgiveness from them?
- Are you still holding on to "bad blood"? *Drop it—it's poison.*
- Do you avoid certain family members because you haven't forgiven them and you don't want them to think you're weak? *It's about God's saving grace, not about you saving face.*

- Is your motto, "I'll never forgive them for that"? *Remember what Jesus reveals in the "Lord's Prayer": "Forgive us our debts, as we also have forgiven our debtors."* (Matthew 6:12)

CHAPTER THIRTEEN

Moving On

AFTER THE SAN FRANCISCO BAY AREA SHOWS, only about three and a half weeks remained in our tour. Where had the time gone? Between enjoying myself so much and working so hard, I never gave much thought to the fantasy being over at some point—too hard a pill to swallow, I guess. With so many cities still awaiting us in those final weeks, I gladly justified delaying taking that pill a little bit longer.

The truth was, the end of the tour meant the end of Ricky and Jada. He never said it would end; I never said it would end; we just knew deep down in our hearts it would end. After all, he lived in Florida, I lived in Tennessee; he never spoke of moving to Tennessee, nor I of moving to Florida.

I suppose a long-distance relationship between two trusting, secure individuals with normal, nine-to-five work hours could work. But that type of relationship certainly didn't describe us. Once back to our respective hometowns, modeling assignments for me and law school for Ricky would fill our schedules, giving us anything but normal nine-to-five work hours.

Did I say: "Trusting and secure individuals"? That certainly wasn't us. Not that Ricky ever gave me real reason not to trust him; but at times, his roaming eyes and flirtatious ways with other women were more than my insecure self could handle. I never told him that, for fear he would accuse me of being jealous and leave me. What a crazy and torturous sort of love! Still, I remained hopeful that our so-called love would stand the test of time and distance.

❦

Raising my head ever so slightly off the pillow while squinting one eye to better focus, I noticed the large six and two zeros displayed on the alarm clock. My fingers fumbled to the snooze button to stifle the annoying beeps that seemed to be growing louder each second. I plopped my head back down, delighted that I could sneak in fifteen more minutes before really needing to get my day started. The chill in the room reminded me of our location: Denver, Colorado. We'd made our way there via Portland, Seattle and Salt Lake City, with a dozen or so other towns nestled in between.

Before dozing back off, my mind fast-forwarded to a quick shopping spree Princess and I planned to have before reporting to our next port of call. As first-time visitors to Colorado, we decided to heed the advice of locals who urged us to take in the mile-long shopping wonders of the 16th Street Mall. The entire city of Denver—with its impressive Red Rock Mountain backdrop and mild temperatures—captured our hearts for the short time we were there. I made a mental note to vacation there sometime.

My mind then rewound to two days ago, replaying yet another pinnacle of my *Ebony Fashion Fair* career. Just before our evening show, I received a call from Mrs. Johnson's assistant informing me that I was selected as a panel shoot model. Flabbergasted and speechless, I wanted to jump through the phone and kiss him!

Anyone who has ever been to an *Ebony Fashion Fair* show during that time period knows that the show's scenery consisted of approximately seventeen panels featuring gigantic pictures of models wearing the latest fashions from top designers around the world. As an added bonus to posing for the panel, those photos could possibly be used on the cover of the *Ebony Fashion Fair* program book, inside an *Ebony* or *Jet* magazine or on a larger-than-life-sized billboard that could be posted anywhere in the United States and Canada. It was hard to imagine my "ugly-as-yo'-momma" face splattered across a larger-than-life poster, but I quickly got used to the idea.

After our show that night, two other selected models and I flew to Chicago. We arose early the next morning, eager for a full day of charming the camera. Confined to the Johnson Publishing Company's photo studio for the entire day, each model shot seven to eight pieces. I enjoyed every minute of that day. The only part I disliked was having to wait weeks to find out which one of my shots would make the cut.

I returned to the tour and began counting down those final days. No one could have prepared me for what came next.

🙾

On May 14, 2000, our exhilarating, successful 1999-2000 season ended in Montreal, Canada. It was time to go home—time to leave Ricky. All the models and crew were dropped off at the Montreal International Airport to board planes headed to all points of the compass. Me to Nashville; Ricky to Gainesville; and Princess to Hollywood to launch her acting career.

There were many tears, hugs and promises to keep in touch. Meeting again on next year's tour was not a sure thing—most models are there for only one year, so those goodbyes were heart-felt. After living and working day-in and day-out with the same people for nine months straight, I couldn't fathom them not being there when I woke up the next morning. I especially couldn't yet imagine the feeling of not waking up in Ricky's arms. Most of my tears went into that good-bye.

Fashion Week was my saving grace for seeing Ricky again soon. In two weeks, Princess, Ricky, myself and a few other models from our tour were booked for the *Fashion Week of the Americas*, held in Miami, Florida. The recipe of success for that much-awaited week: Urban/Latino-flavored fashion shows and exhibits; the amazing creations of twenty-seven designers from fourteen countries; heavy media coverage; and of course, lavish after-parties at the chicest clubs in town tossed in for good measure.

I tried to console myself with the fact that I would see Ricky again soon. We would hang out with each other in between shows and attend each other's shows when possible. It would be wonderful...

Yeah, but my heart didn't buy it—it still grieved. The grief grew from uncertainty. It was the same kind of uncertainty I'd felt when I was ten and my mother, Rece and I moved back to San Pablo and I would lie awake at night wondering if we had enough food to eat the next day. The bare cupboards told me "no," but my determined mind, believing that my mother would come through for us, disputed what my eyes saw.

I mustered up that same dogged determination while standing there, years later, at Montreal International Airport. It didn't matter that Ricky lived seven hundred miles from me. We *would* be together—forever!

✻

What a bittersweet moment, when my eyes caught a glimpse of the morning sun that rushed into my bedroom in Nashville. I instantly noticed the difference between my own skimpy drapes and the hotel's wonderfully heavy, sun-resistant shades; my own bed and the hotel's firm and uninviting bed.

That's right, I'm home! That revelation allowed me to joyfully disregard the sun's attempts to rouse my body from my bed. I turned over for two more hours of much-needed sleep.

I loved being back in the midst of family. I even appreciated the thought of a less hectic schedule for the next several months. Yet I already missed the excited crowds we mingled with before and after the shows, the amazed looks of the audience when we stepped out in some out-of-this-world fashion and the rush I got each time I briskly strolled that runway.

As I stood at the bathroom mirror later that morning—methodically brushing my teeth—my mind raced back over almost every moment of my first nine-month tour with *Ebony Fashion Fair*. How swiftly it had zoomed by; how exhilarating it had been! What wonderful people I'd met; from the famous to the ordinary; from the ones we partied hardy with to the ones who wanted to just touch, get a picture of or an autograph from a "real model."

I took a long stare into that mirror and said out loud, "Wow, I did it!" I congratulated myself and praised God—totally elated to have done it, and done it well.

✻

Enjoyable as it was, that one week back home seemed to crawl by. When Ricky and I finally met at Miami International Airport, we embraced as though it had been years, not days, since seeing each other. I didn't want to let him go—physically, at that moment, nor emotionally. *Why did I dread the relationship ending?* I asked myself. *Why can't I just enjoy the time we have together?*

A little while later, Princess' plane arrived, after which we headed to our hotel. Princess could read the sadness-mixed-with-happiness expression on my face and made it her mission to ensure I had a good time on that trip—free of emotional stress. That first night there, while Ricky prepared for his show the next day, Princess suggested that she and I check out a nightclub we'd discovered a couple of months earlier during our tour. In my opinion, that club was better than any other club I'd been to in terms of ambiance, décor and upscale patrons. During our previous visit there, Princess and I had been in the place barely three minutes when a waiter approached us, carrying a tray with two glasses of wine, announcing it as a gift from the owner of the club. Just as he mentioned something about upstairs, which looked like a VIP section above the bar, the loud music drowned out his words and we strained unsuccessfully to read his lips.

"Thank you. Who's the owner?" Princess queried as she lifted one of the glasses of wine from the tray. He then positioned the tray in front of me and I graciously declined, asking for soda instead. He nodded, acknowledging my drink request, then motioned with his head for us to follow him upstairs, which we did.

Upstairs, in a private, glass-encased room overlooking the lower level stood the club owner, who happened to be an NFL football player. Out rolled the red carpet. Several other players and their women friends hung out in the huge, plush room—eating from a generous buffet and drinking from what seemed to be a bottomless well. After about an hour or so, we left, having invited them to our other shows in the area as an expression of our appreciation.

During Fashion Week, we must have performed about eleven shows: Rocawear, Enyce, Phat Pharm, Baby Phat and Karl Kani, just to name a few. A pleasant surprise came several weeks later when I spotted my picture from one of those shows in *Vibe* magazine (I can't remember what issue), sporting a sexy bikini bottom and jean jacket by Baby Phat. I truly thought I would explode from excitement. I looked hot!

That week in Miami proved a perfect climax to a wonderful season of modeling for me. Perfect, that is, if you don't count the little incident that almost got me killed. I made an important discovery during that trip: the only thing worse than a cheating husband is a cheating husband's angry wife!

Apparently, some salacious gossip stirred regarding Princess and that football player whose nightclub we had just visited. That same guy who told Princess he wasn't married suddenly sprouted a very angry wife. I'm sure that wife had a right to be angry—but at the lying husband, *not* the innocent third party! Even more confusing was the fact that she was angry at *me* too, and I had no part in the whole mix-up!

Ricky's shows were held at different times than Princess' and mine; therefore, she and I were left to fend for ourselves with that angry wife. It seemed like everywhere we went, she appeared out of nowhere—always with her posse, which consisted of five or six wannabes fluttering around her like brainless pigeons, twittering "How high?" when she said "Jump."

One afternoon, I attended Ricky's show alone. I settled into my seat, anticipating my man's promenade across the stage. To my chagrin, that angry wife and her chirping sidekicks sat right behind me, interrupting my enjoyment of the show. They talked plenty of trash—loudly, so that I could hear them. I didn't say a thing, just ignored them as best I could. Still, I heard every word.

"Ho's need to find their own men and leave married ones alone!"

"She gonna catch a bad one hanging 'round Miami."

"They foolin' with the wrong one!"

Their ridiculous jabbering went on for the entire show. I could never understand why my presence threatened that woman. If she were at all observant, she would see my interest rested with Ricky. Every time he came out on the runway I jumped up, snapped pictures and screamed his name. I could care less about her poor excuse for a husband.

After the show, I hurried backstage to wait for Ricky. While waiting, I stepped out in the alley and called Princess to report on our stalker. "Girl, your man's wife's been following me!" I knew that was a cheap shot labeling him as Princess' man, but I really had an attitude about the whole ordeal by that time. I didn't know for sure if anything had transpired between Princess and that football player. I never asked her because I didn't want to know. Those vicious rumors could have been just that—vicious rumors. (In fact, I would find out later that they were.)

"He's not my man, and she's been following me too," Princess snapped back. "Watch out for a cream Lexus with tinted windows."

Just as Princess mentioned that, the cream Lexus sped right into the alley. It screeched to a halt near an entrance to the building next door. As with most alleys, the backs of the buildings all looked alike. They must have thought they stopped at the stage door that led to the models' dressing rooms. They were hunting me down!

"Princess!" I whispered loudly into the phone as I whirled around, turning my back towards the Lexus. "They're here! I gotta go!"

I hung up my cell phone and ran inside just as some of the women piled out of the car. I couldn't believe I was running away from some women over something I had nothing to do with.

When I found Ricky and told him what happened, he laughed—by far not the loving, protective response I desired and needed at the moment. It was not like I wanted him to go out there and beat them up or anything, but a little compassion would have sufficed. Nevertheless, I felt safer just being next to Ricky, so I certainly did not leave his side the rest of the night.

❧

Still indignant over the whole angry wife episode, I didn't bother to call Princess back that night. We'd finished our week of shows and I had a weekend full of one-on-one time with Ricky to look forward to before heading back home. All my attention was on him.

The next afternoon, after banishing my bad attitude toward Princess, I called her on her cell phone only to discover she was already back in Los Angeles!

"What are you doing in L.A.? And why didn't you tell me you were leaving?" I yelled.

She explained that she literally feared for her life when she'd encountered That Woman and her entourage the night I spotted them in the alley. She'd caught a red-eye flight as fast as she could out of Miami. I didn't blame her one bit.

The irony is we both departed that city with fear in our hearts. Albeit under different circumstances, in both cases, involvement with a man spawned that fear.

BE-You-TIFUL
TRINITY

Lessons on Life
PRACTICAL APPLICATION

There was a time in my life when I found myself following other people. I was following my friends, my boyfriend and the hope of acceptance. I wasn't doing what I knew I should do. I only wanted to be a part of the crowd.

It only takes one negative thought to produce a bad decision, and it only takes one bad decision to delay or destroy a promising future. The way to approach any decision in life is to count the cost before you get excited about the profit margin.

I remember times in my travel with *Ebony Fashion Fair* that I would end up in "bad" places despite my best judgment. On some occasions this would prove dangerous or even life threatening. I can truly say that if it wasn't for God's mercy and the teaching I got from my mentors, I would be in a world of hurt today.

To truly exercise your "best judgment," you need to remember that you are not just a body. You have a spirit that translates God's inspiration to the body through the intellect, and when the body reacts to this, it affects the soul. You can't achieve true wholeness without a clear understanding of all three entities.

As much as we would like to be validated by such things, we are not defined by what we do for a living, our accumulated wealth or even what we have failed to accumulate. Although these things are a part of our lives, our reality is spiritual.

Good Things Come in Threes

Here's a trinity of life lessons that I had to learn the hard way.

Life lesson #1: Ask questions if you want answers.
Ask questions. Listen carefully to the answers with an open mind, an open heart and a willing and obedient spirit. Asking the right questions will make your life so much easier. You won't always do the right things even when you have all the answers, but you'll have a higher success rate if you do. You are only as strong as you are humble, and you are only as smart as the question you're humble enough to ask.

Fail to ask questions and you can only take steps backward into uncertainty. Ask questions and you can move forward with knowledge.

Can you really afford *not* to ask questions? Can you function effectively without true answers? Don't forget that the best person to ask is God.

Life lesson #2: Study to learn.
There is no such thing as being finished with learning. As long as you live, you will be learning, whether for good or evil. You should never just hand over your mind to someone without carefully researching the facts for yourself. It is important to study hard so that you will have the information you need to make sound decisions.

Just because someone gives you an answer doesn't mean it's factual. You wouldn't just eat what a perfect stranger put before you. If you did, you'd be putting your health at risk. You'd want to know something about the food and the person who provided it.

Find out for yourself if the food is good for you, and make sure you can trust the cook!

Life lesson # 3: Get ready for your test.
You may choose to avoid asking questions or searching for answers, but keep this in mind: As long as you live, you will always be faced with tests. You'll only pass those tests if you've studied the material.

CHAPTER FOURTEEN

Stepping Up to the Plate

ONE WEEK LATER—after my nerves calmed from the Miami drama—I flew to Boston and began classes at Emerson College. I purposed in my heart to be a television broadcaster; and that summer, a door opened up to help me with that dream. When our show had taken us to Boston several months earlier, I'd had the good fortune of meeting Karen Holmes Ward, host and producer for *City Line*, an award-winning urban news and feature magazine program in Boston.

Ms. Holmes offered me the opportunity to intern with that ABC-TV affiliate program, and I jumped at the challenge. *Thank you, God!*

One day, while sitting at my desk at the TV station, I received a call on my cell phone from Mrs. Johnson—not her assistant, but Mrs. Johnson herself. That caught me off guard; so much so that I nervously scrambled from my desk and headed outside to continue my conversation there. *Why in the world am I nervous?* I wondered. *Only great things have happened to my career because of this woman; what was there to be uneasy about now?*

I suspected my nervousness was a result of the deep respect I had for Mrs. Eunice W. Johnson—not just because of the promotions that had come my way through her, but simply for her embodiment of excellence. I have never known another woman to put so much emphasis on and effort into making great things happen in an honorable way. Those same characteristics are found in her husband as well, but Mrs. Johnson is the one I worked most closely with, so I saw the results of her work daily.

"Jada," she said, "would you like to go to Paris and Rome with me?"

"Of course, I would *love* to go," I responded, even before the realization of what she asked settled in.

"Where are you now?"

"I'm in Boston."

"What are you doing in Boston?"

"Attending school and interning at Channel 5."

"Oh, well I wouldn't want to take you away from your schooling."

"Oh no, I would rather go to Paris and Rome."

"Well, I tell you what; you think it over, and I'll do the same. I'll call you back tomorrow."

Decisions, decisions! I had never been to Europe, so to be able to travel there and get a first-hand look at the top designers' apparel for the upcoming season seemed like a no-brainer. On the other hand, the tremendous amount of broadcasting I had yet to learn at Emerson overwhelmed me, making me think I needed to stay and tackle all the classes I could in the short time left during the summer.

I had already been asked back to the next *Ebony Fashion Fair* tour, starting up again in September. It was a huge, humbling honor, to say the least, but at the same time, it would be a major interruption of my broadcasting dreams and a huge downward spiral in my relationship with Ricky.

Even though no talk of marriage or long-term commitment ever came up, Ricky seemed to assume that I would settle down in Florida with him. He never exactly said what he saw as the "big picture" for our relationship, but it certainly angered him to learn that I'd accepted an opportunity to go back on the road. He obviously had no clue how much my career had progressed from the moment I began that 1999 *Ebony Fashion Fair* tour.

Or maybe he did know, which is what made him so angry.

Was Ricky jealous? I immediately erased that thought. After all, why should a husband or boyfriend ever be jealous of his woman? He should be happy to see her excelling in her career, as it only benefits both of them in the long run. But that was the main problem with Ricky—he wasn't my husband, and things were beginning to look shaky as far as him even being my boyfriend.

Things seemed to change from the moment Ricky knew I'd be going back on tour. He appeared to be sneaking around during the time we were apart. Even though I never actually caught him cheating on me, I always sensed that he did. Maybe the fact that he began holding back on his emotions tipped me off. I wasn't able to put much time and thought into romance though, with my career so demanding of me. I put in long, hard hours most days—if not on a class project, then on an assignment at the TV station. I prayed my relationship would just fix itself.

Word to the wise: that trick never works.

※

My duties at *City Line* ran the gamut from researching story ideas, booking guests and writing show promotions, to actually writing and producing a long-format piece for broadcast. I remember my first writing project featured the re-make of the movie, *Shaft*, in which Samuel L. Jackson delivered an awesome performance.

The project most dear to me—the one I wrote and produced in its entirety—dealt with teens and low self-esteem. I selected that topic for obvious reasons. I wanted to dig deep into the cause of low self-esteem in order to offer solace and solution to millions of others who had grown up with rejection.

I interviewed well-known psychologists in the Boston area—namely, Alvin Poussaint, one of the advisors for "The Cosby Show." My story was helped a lot by his knowledge of the actions and reactions of adolescents moving into adulthood. I had no idea of the many revelations I would encounter during my extensive investigation of that story—revelations that would shed tremendous light on my relationship with my parents.

One of the most noteworthy revelations for me was that I could not *find* self-esteem. I had to *build* it.

The second revelation: parents are a critical catalyst in esteem building. High self-esteem—or just plain healthy feelings about oneself—starts in the home and is actually cultivated in children from birth.

It is truly amazing how our minds are shaped as we develop. No matter if you're a child or an adult, the key to life is not *who* teaches us what we know or *where* learning takes place in our lives, but rather that we continue in our own search for the truth.

We should never trust what we've learned in the past without seeking its true meaning for our future. It's easy for us blame our parents or even ourselves for some of the pratfalls we've taken in life, but we must keep in mind that the gift of learning is ours for the taking. It is up to us to receive what has been freely given to us. Our mistakes reveal our ignorance, but continuing in our search for wisdom can shield us from the worst consequences of that ignorance. Parents and friends were never meant to guide us past all of life's obstacles—only God can do that. We must remember what Scripture says of Jesus: that He is the Author and Perfecter of our faith (Hebrews 12:2).

The sad truth is that most parents remain so messed up due to their own parents not bringing *them* up right, that they never come close to getting it right with their own offspring. I suppose some people—as in the case of my own parents—just never learn that they *should* do it, let alone *how* it ought to be done.

Subconsciously, I'd been pointing the finger at my parents for all my problems in life. *But why did I still blame them after so many years?*

※

Producing that story conjured up a slew of memories. I'd faced challenges with low self-esteem as early as the fourth grade after my family moved to a predominantly white community. That was when I realized I was "too"- too tall, too dark, with too-kinky hair. I wanted my hair to be straight and silky. I desired pale skin. I longed for the automatic acceptance that my classmates enjoyed just by being the majority. They seemed to be accepted by all; the best I could expect was acceptance by some.

Experts in the study of self-esteem will tell you that children intuitively mirror others' perception of them—good or bad. They measure themselves by the standards set by those outside forces shaping their lives. That very thing happened to me from the fourth grade on. Presented with the notion that black wasn't good enough, I wanted to be white.

I vividly recalled the day a boy in the fourth grade reported loudly— as a bunch of us stood around at recess—that his mother told him to never pick a black girl for a girlfriend. As he pointed to me and laughed, his friends joined in; so did my so-called girlfriends. The scars of rejection run deep as evidenced by the fact that I remembered the details of that minor incident so many years later.

It perhaps wasn't so much the actual statement by his mother that bothered me as a child. After all, hadn't I heard that same sort of command from my own father? Hadn't he threatened Rece and I a dozen times (if not more) with, "Don't come home with a white boy"? No, the real problem wasn't the context of the statement; it was the fact that the boy received that negative statement, took ownership of it and used it to hurt another person. I know now, without a doubt, that his word weaponry would not have even grazed my skin if I'd been sure of my own self-worth.

The third and most eye-opening revelation I had during the production of that show was that positive self-worth is critical in achieving a prosperous life. The type of prosperity I'm referring to is the kind that is achieved with a "prosperous" mind, not by acquiring "things." Persons with this type of mindset, with this type of healthy self-esteem, are more capable of making decisions without being fearful of the outcome. They are capable of offering thanks, not apologies, for their accomplishments. They are more willing to take responsibility for all their actions—good or bad. And they can better cope with stressful situations. I wanted that for myself.

I had a final and faith-filled epiphany: forgiveness is vital to overcoming low self-esteem. Most people would not even consider forgiveness a factor, but it is. Over the years, placing blame on my parents became a natural thing to do—an easy thing to do. Experts even validated such action on my part. But in doing so, it absolved me of all responsibility for being who I was. It kept me from taking ownership of my actions. Therefore, I had to now question why I was blaming others for my pain. In questioning myself, I realized there was one thing I had to do—forgive!

Until I forgave my father and mother, I continued to blame them. As long as I blamed them, I continued to look at myself through their eyes. As long as I looked at myself through their eyes, I didn't like what I saw; hence, low self-esteem. That principle applied to not just my parents but to anyone else whose encounter with me was not positive.

Right then and there, I forgave my parents for their neglect, abuse and lack of knowledge of how to raise me. I forgave all my classmates for any acts of prejudice against me—witting or unwitting. I especially forgave the entire male gender for letting me down so many times and so many ways. Last but not least, I forgave myself for harboring such hatred in my heart for my parents and everyone else. It felt good to forgive! It felt good to be on my way to recovery!

※

Mrs. Johnson called me back as scheduled, instructing me, in a motherly fashion, to complete my summer classes and internship. She promised to include me in the Europe trip next year. Who was I to argue with her? Next summer sounded good enough for me.

Before we got off the phone, Mrs. Johnson said, "By the way, Jada, I want you to come to Chicago for a day and help me with the auditions for the upcoming season."

"Sure!" I almost squealed. "What day should I be there?"

She said her secretary would call me with the date, which she did about three hours later. While jotting down the information in my date book, it reminded me that I needed to finalize my flight plans to Florida. I planned to visit Ricky before having to report for my second season with *Ebony Fashion Fair*.

I called Ricky, anxious to talk about my trip to Florida to see him, but even more anxious to share with him the news about the auditions. Although I didn't expect him to be as excited as I was, I did expect him to be happy for me. His congratulations were lukewarm at best. He wasn't impressed one little bit that I'd received all my good news from Mrs. Johnson personally.

I hung up from the call perplexed. *Was* Ricky jealous of my achievements? Was that why he didn't seem to want for me the same things I wanted for myself? The thought bothered me…a lot.

Three weeks later, I arrived at the Johnson Publishing Company headquarters for a very full day of body assessments, strut and pivot evaluations, and even attitude analysis for approximately sixty *Ebony Fashion Fair* wanna-bes. They came in every shape, size, color and attitude: Light-skinned, dark-skinned, muscular, curvaceous and boney. Confident, arrogant and insecure. In all that diversity, however, there remained one common denominator: they all arrived hungry for a spot on the tour.

It seemed like only yesterday I'd stood in their shoes. In the midst of that reflection, I thanked God that I was on the other side of the judging table. Because I could relate to the stress those models were going through, I extended a warm smile to them whenever possible to help calm their nerves. But for the most part, I suppose my smile wasn't just for their sake; it simply appeared spontaneously, thanks to having just received the most exciting news of my life…

Earlier that morning, I'd arrived at O'Hare Airport. Steve, the stage manager, met me at the gate. I was happy to see him. Not just because being in

Boston by myself for almost three months had left me craving family, friends, coworkers or anyone I knew well enough to hang out with, but because I had actually grown very fond of Steve over the past year.

When I'd been dubbed assistant commentator that previous fall—with no indication of what to do with that auspicious title—Steve had taken me under his wing and coached me along as though I already had real commentating duties. In fact, if it weren't for his guidance and confidence-building pep talks, I would not have been as ready as I was in Alabama several months later when asked to stand in at a moment's notice.

"There have been some changes J," he'd said almost immediately after we hugged and greeted each other.

"What kind of changes?"

Steve grabbed my carry-on bag from me and we headed toward the exit. "Well, our commentator quit."

"What do you mean?" As I spoke those words, my feet froze to the floor; my purse slid off my shoulder and I stood waiting for Steve to realize I was no longer walking beside him.

"She quit. She's not coming back," he turned and came back a few steps to where I stood gawking at him. With no further explanation to offer, he stooped down, picked up my purse and gently placed it back on my shoulder. "I just wanted to prepare you because Mrs. Johnson is going to offer you the commentator position today."

Obviously, the news caught me off guard. I remained speechless. My brain did, however, give me the signal to immediately rejoice over the news, so I grinned from ear to ear and planted the biggest kiss on Steve's cheek. He kissed me back and added a hug to it as well. As I celebrated on the outside, I said a special prayer on the inside for my predecessor. Not knowing the reason behind her leaving, I prayed all was okay for her.

Sure enough, as soon as I saw Mrs. Johnson, she took me to the side and asked me if I would be interested in taking over the commentator position. For a second time—just like when she'd told me almost a year ago that I'd made the swimsuit edition—I wanted to fall down at her feet in some drastic display of gratitude. Instead, I opted for a much more reserved demeanor: a smile and a firm, "Yes, I would."

That was that. There was not a lot of time to grasp hold of what had really happened, as it was then time to rush off to conduct the auditions. In the blink of an eye, that mid-July morning in 2000, I became "Jada Jackson, Commentator for the *Ebony Fashion Fair*."

BE-You-TIFUL
TRINITY

Revelation Connection
PRACTICAL APPLICATION

One of the most life-changing revelations came to me while working on a self-esteem project in Boston entitled "Insecurity and Low Self-esteem." The project intrigued me because I was in search of answers for myself about these things. As my research continued, these words leapt out at me again and again—*insecurity and low self-esteem.*

Although I could identify with the moral affects of these terms, I wasn't sure what caused them and how they might be healed. At this point in my life, I'm an avid believer that healing from any moral and spiritual disease begins with connecting to the Source of healing. I'm talking about Jesus Christ. He is the Way, the Truth and the Life—the Divine Physician.

If you feel unloved, you need to connect with love in order to reap the benefits of love. If you feel rejected, you need to disconnect with negative people and connect with healthier relationships and positive environments. If you feel worthless, you need to connect with someone who will show his or her appreciation for you. The key to fulfillment and wholeness in daily life is your connection with your spiritual Life.

The only reason I felt low, depleted and worthless was because I was burying myself in my own issues rather than submerging myself in the real purpose of life.

Check Your Connections

Here are three things for you to meditate on as you grapple with your own issues of self-worth:

1. **What are you connected to?**
   - Are you connected more to your pain than your purpose? *Be careful of becoming selfish and self-consumed.*
   - Are you connected to someone because of what they can give you instead of what you can offer them? *Be aware of your need to feel accepted.*
   - Are you connected to a group or organization that doesn't promote God's way? *Be watchful for "wolves in sheep's clothing." Remember: they're known by their fruits.*

2. **Things you should disconnect from.**
   - Learn from your past, but disconnect from the hurt and pain of it. *Guard against becoming angry and bitter.*
   - Disconnect from self-images that remind you of harmful people or situations from your past. *Guard against negative forces and spiritual strongholds.*
   - Disconnect from what you want and be patient about the things you need. *Guard against falling into greed and envy.*

3. **Things you should re-connect to.**
   - **Re-connect with God and your family.** God instituted the family. If family is important to God, then it should be just as important to us.
   - **Re-connect with your true friends, no matter what it takes.** These are the people who love you and value you for who you truly are, not for what you have or what you represent.
   - **Re-connect to the truth.** We have been given an elixir to heal spiritual disease: truth. Lies bring you down; truth lifts you up.

CHAPTER FIFTEEN

Letting Go

As I entered my second season with *Ebony Fashion Fair*, anxiety and excitement overwhelmed me. I was more fired up than I'd been even my first year. There I stood, in front of the Johnson Publishing Company building with an ignited flame of passion in my soul to take on the commentator's role.

Familiarity does have its merits. With so many new models to learn, I felt blessed to see some recognizable faces among the crew members. Since the *Ebony Fashion Fair* models typically only tour for one season, it was not uncommon to have a dozen new models to train all over again.

My mind rewound to Day One of last year's tour when I, myself, had been positioned at the starting blocks. I thought about the first time I met Princess. I missed her. She and I had just joyfully reminisced over the phone several days earlier when I called her with the news of being made the commentator. We laughed about our previous nine-month tour. Boy, had we taken some risks in our quest for fun! Reflecting on all that, I suddenly felt older, wiser and more responsible.

Also facing me in that second season were the familiar runways to be mastered; yet I would master them from a brand new position. Unfortunately, no Commentator's Handbook or a "How-To" guide came with that position. Common sense, on-the-job-training and Steve as an awesome mentor was my entire strategy for success.

They hired Rodney back and he was a lifesaver! He and I worked well together and became best friends in the process. The main thing I loved about Rodney—and the very thing the other models disliked about him—

was his straightforwardness. He was blunt to the point of tactlessness. You never had to guess where he was coming from; you knew up front. His aggressive personality bred controversy, but his expertise led me victoriously through that first year of commentating.

�֍

My shaky relationship with Ricky—now a *distant*, shaky relationship—added a whole new dimension to the new touring season. Between the demands of my work life and the perils of my personal life, I resembled an emotional thermometer with its mercury out of whack, registering extreme temperatures as we moved through the season. Some days I wanted to cry like a baby; other days I wanted to kill like a crazed maniac.

Ricky had decided to stay in Florida and finish his law degree, as opposed to furthering his modeling career at that time. Spending little time together that summer (his law studies in Gainesville and my internship in Boston kept us from visiting each other at all) strained our relationship, to say the least. For some reason—which I now know to be the Spirit of Christ in me trying to guide me to safety against my own stubborn will—I sensed deceitfulness on Ricky's part when it came to women. I'd confronted him about it, but he'd responded with lies; lies I believed.

After all, even though I was not really in love, but just in love with the thought of being in love, I wanted to enjoy the fantasy. Okay, so our relationship was not working from a distance. What, then, would be the solution? What would *any* illogical, desperate, lovesick, insecure young woman do to fix the problem of a straying, lying, cheating boyfriend? You guessed it—we moved in together. Being right there, where I could "change" him, made the most sense to me at that time. Looking back, I can only laugh at my self-righteousness; however, living through that ordeal was no laughing matter.

After moving in with Ricky in Orlando in March 2001, whenever I had a day off from the tour, I flew home to be with him and set up our new apartment. During one of my visits home, a girl called and I happened to answer the phone. The caller sounded baffled at my voice, claiming she must have the wrong number.

"Who are you looking for?" I jumped in before she could hang up.

"Ricky," she said innocently, most likely hoping I was Ricky's sister or his cleaning lady.

My heart stopped as she said his name. I wanted to die. Anyone who has been a victim of infidelity can tell you, it is one thing to have suspicions about your partner cheating; it is something else again to be slapped in the face with it. That was my first encounter, and it cut my heart like a knife. I kept my cool, though, at least long enough to get off the phone.

"No, Ricky's not here," I said, levelly, "but I'll tell him you called. What's your name?" I decided to play the role of sister or cousin just to get what I wanted: evidence.

"That's okay, I'll just call back later." *Click*. She sounded a little upset, as though she may have been on to me, but who cares? *She* was messing with *my* man! The only one who deserved to be offended and angry was me.

I began catching snippets of innuendo in my circle of friends about Ricky hanging out with some of the models from last year. Maybe I'd heard it before, but my eyes and ears were still shut tight to the truth. I hadn't given it much thought before, other than that we all became friends during those nine months of touring and they were just continuing to hang out as friends. At this point in my life, my spirit was awakened to what was really going on; and I was pretty sure those weren't just friendly encounters.

One day while home for a short break, I picked up the mail as I returned from running errands. Ricky's cell phone bill was among the stack. I took the opportunity and read through his itemized bill before going into the apartment. Even though I went looking for it, it hurt like crazy to actually see the evidence. The same number that had showed up on our Caller ID when I answered that girl's call also showed up approximately twenty-five times on that cell phone bill.

My confrontation with Ricky over the matter triggered an explosion. He accused me of being insecure and conniving, labeling his innocent friendship with a helpful classmate as a love affair. As part of his strategy, he became the purported victim in our relationship—being falsely blamed and having his privacy invaded. In my naivety, I fell for his trickery and backed off from nagging him about the phone calls.

My failure to confront him about his disloyalty did not erase those doubts from my mind, though. In fact, in spite of my compromise, the phone calls continued perhaps for another year. That did wonders to increase my insecurity, which in turn, caused us to grow further apart. We argued a lot about other petty things, knowing all along what was at the heart of it all.

How ironic that my relationship with Ricky would mimic my mother and father's! Why didn't I see it coming? Why couldn't I just get out of it? For the first time in my life, I felt deep down, sincere sympathy for Momma and all that she'd endured. I wanted to call her and tell her that I now understood what she'd been through. I guess in some way, I wanted to cry out for help from her too, but I just couldn't bring myself to do that.

※

That summer, Mrs. Johnson kept her promise and called to tell me to pack my bags for Paris and Rome. She has always been a woman of her word and I highly respect her for that to this day. She gave me a tremendous gift that summer—not just the opportunity to go to Paris and Rome, but a real role model. Through Mrs. Johnson, I learned how important it was to keep the promises I made.

On the other hand, I grimaced at the thought of leaving Ricky's side once again. Since Ricky's complaints all along centered on the lack of time I spent with him, I looked forward to just being home after the tour, to give him the attention he desired and deserved. Being so insecure in our relationship, I also feared that being that far away was an open invitation for him to cheat.

My decision to go on that trip proved one of the hardest in my life because deep down, I knew it signified the beginning of the end of the Jada-Ricky chapter in my life.

On July 7, 2001, I stepped onto that plane to Europe, hoping for a breath of much-needed fresh air in my life, one that would sweep away the old, stale atmosphere of insecurity.

※

I'll never forget my first taste of Paris—the language, the food, the designers and all their fabulous creations. We attended every major fashion show in the city to select clothes for our upcoming *Ebony Fashion Fair* season. What a great introduction to the best that Paris had to offer! I never wanted it to end.

Using my traveler's dictionary, I communicated in French whenever possible, making every attempt to fit in. I even wanted to indulge in their fabulous food, but chose to guard against that scrumptious bread served at every meal. In the fashion world, critics' eyes are forever on the models. Whether we are performing or not, we are expected to look super-real—thinner, lighter—as if we floated above the sidewalks. Talk of a big photo shoot at the end of our week-long visit also motivated me to watch what I ate.

Although I focused as much as I possibly could on my role as a buyer, I felt a strong longing for the runway. That longing came partly from observing the amazing designs and beautiful models, some of whom I recognized from magazines and other runways. It also came from observing many novice models, who blundered often and displayed a lack of stage sense.

During one of the shows, I stood by myself off to the side of the stage instead of sitting in the audience. Checking out the models from a commentator's angle rather than a spectator's often gave me a much better perspective of what I needed to look for.

I should be up there! I thought to myself. *I'm as good as the experienced ones and definitely better than most of the novices.*

"Excuse me," came a voice to my left. I turned to see that the voice belonged to a beautiful French woman holding a clipboard.

"Why aren't you in the show?" she continued with a warm smile before I could even say hello.

I just smiled modestly and shrugged my shoulders, although I really wanted to blurt out how much better I believed myself to be than those currently on stage.

"I work for a modeling agency here in Paris and would love for you to come see me." She skillfully flipped her business card out of her tailored jacket pocket—as though she'd done so a hundred times already that day—handed it to me, then proceeded backstage.

"Thank you. I'll consider that," I barely got a chance to tell her that before she whisked back to her models. I kept her card in a safe place, as I didn't want to ever dismiss the possibility of international modeling.

※

I returned home two weeks later to pure hell. I could not have imagined my life with Ricky to get any worse, but it did. Having the shoulders of several girlfriends to cry on—especially my good friend Dereka, a former *Ebony Fashion Fair* model—worked wonders in helping me keep my sanity. One time, Dereka even threatened to hop on a plane from Chicago to

Orlando to strangle Ricky upon finding out he'd locked me out of our apartment in my underwear during an argument.

We lasted another eight months, finally breaking up that following spring. I believe the only reason we continued that long was out of sheer convenience. With me back on the road for my third *Ebony Fashion Fair* season, I had no reason to go out apartment hunting. Also, with me being constantly on the road, Ricky got what he wanted: freedom to sleep around.

We had been together for two-and-a-half years when I packed up my belongings and moved into a one-room apartment at Studio Plus on the grounds of Universal Studios. I remained there for four months until it was time to hit the road again for season number four.

During those four months, I was swamped by loneliness and depression. I didn't have anyone in Orlando to hang out with because I moved there knowing only Ricky, then traveled too much to build any friendships. Pride would not let me go back home to Mom because she'd objected to me moving in with Ricky in the first place. In my arrogant and defiant way, I'd ignored her warning and now couldn't bear having her say, "I told you so."

※

I resumed my course studies that summer, taking some acting classes to help lighten my spirits. When not attending classes, I spent a lot of time deeply searching my soul. I desperately wished I could go back and unmake all my bad decisions. One-and-a-half years ago, it didn't seem like a bad decision to live with a man I believed loved me and would marry me. But the problem with that line of reasoning—used by so many other young women—is that I would make any excuse to satisfy my desires. Sure, that reasoning *seems* sound, but it's phantom reasoning—you don't stand a ghost of a chance of it holding up under real-life stress.

What I wouldn't give to have heeded Mom's advice—to see other young people heed the advice of their elders at major crossroads in life. I could have avoided all kinds of disappointments, setbacks and, in some cases, real harm.

I also spent time repenting to God of my sin of premarital sex-another very bad choice made by giving in to my selfish desires. I had walked away from God and all the truth and understanding of Christian principles that Mom instilled in me over the years. In my hard-headed way, I just wanted to experience life and thought I could handle the route I chose. I never once stopped to think about the cost of those choices. The cost is your soul—the essence of who you are. When you enter into intercourse with another person, it doesn't just involve your physical body—your entire, vulnerable soul gets tangled up with that person. Such an important point to consider, yet so often ignored, especially in the heat of passion.

That's why I knew I had to spend time praising and thanking God for His mercy! He'd saved me from so many terrible consequences of my sins. I could have gotten pregnant, forcing me to raise a child out of wedlock, bringing my modeling career to a sudden halt. I could have contracted a sexually transmitted disease, even AIDS, possibly bringing my very life to a sudden halt. I'd opened the door and issued an invitation for a number of bad things to happen; the only reason they didn't was the sheer grace of God!

Last but not least, I spent a lot of time getting my heart right before God. That entailed forgiving Ricky.

In a conversation we'd had months prior, he apologized for lying to me about the "other girl" who continued to call him over and over and over again. He told me that he just let it go too far. He wanted to get back together, he said.

I just couldn't do it. I had to do what was right for me. He'd lied to me and deceived me on so many occasions. But none of that mattered now. I had to forget what he'd done and forgive him. The Bible says that if we do not forgive others for their trespasses, God will not forgive us for ours. I already felt that Mom was gravely disappointed in me because I went astray, and knew I was suffering the consequences of my actions. I didn't want to let Mom down any more, and I certainly wanted God's forgiveness. In my heart, I forgave Ricky that very moment. It felt really good, like the world had been lifted from my shoulders.

For the first time in my life, I realized in my spirit that God has a distinct purpose and plan for me on this earth. Obedience on my part would be required to see that plan to completion. I immediately rededicated my life to God and told Him I was willing to do things *His* way, not mine.

There *was* life after Ricky. And I knew I would be just fine in it.

BE-You-TIFUL
TRINITY

Letting Go & Cutting Your Losses
PRACTICAL APPLICATION

How do we know when to retreat? When I made the decision to leave Ricky, it was the hardest thing I'd ever done. Even though I had proof of his unfaithfulness, I still felt compelled to be loyal to him.

If you're going to invest your time and effort into something or someone, it only makes sense that you know everything you can about your investment. One or two years is a long time to be in a relationship and not be sure of your partner's intentions and fidelity.

Over and over again, as my relationship with Ricky deteriorated, I asked myself: *Why can't I just walk away and cut my losses? Why do I refuse to face the truth when I can see that he's lied?*

I came to understand that the longer you stay connected to something or someone, the more attached you become. For this reason, it's necessary for us to stay connected to God, because if we're connected to the truth, it's easier to see the lie and where it leads. It's easier to detach ourselves from the lie when we can see it clearly.

A good investor is mentally and financially prepared for the worst to happen and knows when to cut his or her losses. Life is not a game of chance; we shouldn't gamble with what God has entrusted us to manage. You wouldn't take blind risks with your money—why would you take them with your life? When it comes to relationships, you can't afford to take blind risks. That's why it's so important to *know* the people you call "friends"—not just what's lying on the surface, but the real people underneath.

Bad Investments

What are you investing your life in? Is your investment a benefit or liability?

There are three things that can go wrong because of a bad investment of your precious life energies and resources. A bad investment can:

1. Tap out your resources.

Some relationships are motivated by a spirit of greed or lust and only benefit one party. How do you know if you're in such a relationship? You'll find you're suffering loss in one or more of three main areas in your life:

- Finances
- Emotions
- Health

A relationship in which the other party behaves in ways that deplete these resources is a liability. It will never be spiritually profitable for you.

The first step to cutting your losses is to recognize and acknowledge the damage that has been done to your life.

2. Put you and others at risk.

In general, I don't consider establishing relationships with people a risk, but I've learned that if you don't fully know a person's character, pursuing a lifetime commitment with them is a high-risk venture.

Most risks that turn out badly don't just affect *you*. In the end, they harm anyone emotionally connected to you as well. Don't just think of yourself when it comes to your resources, your time and your well-being.

If you've walked blindly into a risky relationship, you're putting other people's resources on the line, too.

3. Bring about total loss.

As I said earlier, a bad decision can be disastrous or even fatal. I once knew someone who got involved with an investment deal that turned out to be a scam. They lost all their money and later died from a massive heart attack.

There's such a thing as "high risk behavior." Smoking cigarettes causes illness that can lead to death. Marrying someone you barely know and starting a family with them can result in you finding yourself a lonely and stressed out single parent. I'm not saying that you'll never suffer loss if you're careful, nor am I suggesting that you should live in fear of making decisions, *but it can be a matter of life and death when you get involved in something without God's direction.*

CHAPTER SIXTEEN

Ernest

I MENTALLY PREPARED TO WIND DOWN THE summer course studies and don my commentator hat for the 2002-2003 season. There was a new light before me that illuminated my path—the path that God set forth for me. I didn't know all the answers, couldn't see what lay ahead or around the corners, but I trusted my Navigator. God said it would be good. He said that if I meditated on and lived my life according to His Word, He would make my crooked paths straight (and boy, don't we all have some crooked paths).

Before I'd discovered God's roadmap, I kept trying to straighten those paths through my own ability, wondering why I failed to do it over and over. What a relief to finally know it would all be handled correctly!

A week before heading to Chicago, my god-brother, Mano, a keyboard player for gospel artist, Kurt Karr, invited me to a concert. Their band was performing at the Orange County Convention Center as part of the Judah Conference—an annual Christian music conference sponsored by Clint Brown Ministries.

I am forever grateful to Mano for my presence at that conference, where I sang and worshipped uninhibitedly. Many people that night responded to the call for Jesus to fulfill His vision in their lives. That spiritually refreshing and encouraging atmosphere left me more certain than ever of my own recent recommitment to Him.

Afterwards, I floated along with the flow of people pouring out into the lobby like a slow-moving stream emptying into a large, calm lake. No one wanted the concert to be over. I slumped exhaustedly on a bench near a side entrance where my brother and I had planned to meet. Even though my body felt worn out from all the energy I'd spent, my spirit still greatly rejoiced to those powerful songs dancing through my head.

Fortunately for me, the majority of the lingering crowd congregated on the other side of the lobby, for I liked the private concert going on in my head and dared anyone to disturb it. I closed my eyes and leaned back against the wall to better reflect on the whole evening.

I never knew Mano played so well. His group had impressed me; the whole conference impressed me. I made a mental note to check out Clint Brown's church, FaithWorld, the next time I was home from the tour. I chuckled to myself at the use of the word "home." Was Orlando my home? Nothing there *felt* like home anymore. Come to think about it, had it ever?

Lord, I know I'm on the right track with my life right now, but just where are You leading me?

"What's your name?"

I quickly figured out that that smooth, sweet voice was not God responding to my question, and therefore considered it an uninvited interruption to my personal praise session. I opened my eyes and flashed the voice's owner a stoned-faced look, letting him know without words that I didn't appreciate being bothered. Even though I had forgiven Ricky for deceiving me, a bad taste remained in my mouth when I thought about men. I know that forgetting is supposed to go hand-in-hand with forgiving, but God would just have to be patient with me on that one. Too many bad moments had played out between Ricky and I for me to just forget them all so soon.

Why, God, do those memories pop up out of the clear blue every time I meet a man?

Truth is, I would have gotten up and moved away from the intruder when he first asked my name had he not looked so sweet and innocent and exuded such loving warmth. It seemed as though the fiery darts that projected from my eyes ricocheted from a huge shield of love surrounding this guy. I had never experienced that sensation before in my life. His whole essence was non-threatening and inviting.

He boldly but gently repeated his question, oblivious to my fiery darts. "What's your name?"

"I'm Jada," came my sweet reply. Where did *that* come from? I surprised myself. I was supposed to be disturbed and irritated, but somehow those emotions evaporated. *Humph. An impressive touch.*

"Do you live in Orlando?" He was really pushing, not giving me a chance to even ask him his name.

"Yeah," I responded hesitantly, trying to figure where he was going with this conversation.

"Are you saved?"

Oh, please, you've got to be kidding me. I've never heard that pick-up line before. Where is this guy from? Is he serious?

As he stood waiting for an answer, I knew he was very serious indeed. Bold, but refreshing.

"Yeah, I'm saved! Are you?" I shot back. *Oh, I can't believe I said that!*

The man merely smiled at my attack and nodded his head. Accurately assuming that I had never been asked that question by a stranger at a concert, he proceeded to put me at ease by telling me he was the keyboard player in Clint Brown's band. Just as he reached into his bag to pull out their latest CD, Mano walked up. The two of them shook hands and greeted each other, making small talk about band stuff—obviously acquaintances.

Okay, so he's a born-again believer, sweet person, very cute and now I find out he knows my brother. Things are really stacking up in his favor!

"So, Jada, you've met Ernest, huh?" Mano assumed as he turned to me.

I stood—a hint that I was ready to leave. "Well, actually…" I stammered, a little embarrassed that I'd never asked the man his name.

"Pardon me for not properly introducing myself. I'm Ernest Collins and it's been a pleasure talking to you. Can I have your phone number?"

The audacity of him—asking for my number in the same breath he tells me his name, and in front of my brother! As much as I wanted Ernest to be different than Ricky, his request for my phone number echoed the other thirty or so requests I'd received since splitting up with Ricky. I hesitated, thinking, *This guy could end up being just like all the rest, except for his unique Jesus-talk cover up.* But then again, I liked his boldness. Wrapped up in that boldness, I thought I saw a genuine God-kind-of-love that I'd never experienced in any other man. How could I resist?

I dug in my purse for some paper and a pen and quickly scrawled out my number. I handed it to him with a smile and a hope that my better judgment would not fail me this time. As Mano and I walked in one direction and Ernest in another, he held up that piece of paper and promised to call me real soon.

He called the very next day. Major point in his favor: a man who keeps his word. I actually looked forward to conversing with him once more, so when he invited me to dinner that night, I gave a nonchalant acceptance while inside, I could hardly contain my excitement.

The evening started slowly, with Ernest proving to be a man of few words. I undertook the arduous task of getting him to say more than ten things in the first hour we were together. It was a challenge, and I soon opted to tell him (or warn him) about my recent exit from a bad relationship. I suppose my approach—laying all my cards on the table as first-date dialogue—showed a true lack of dating skills on my part.

Being the gentleman that he was, Ernest took it all in stride. In fact, at one point during my rehashing when it really sounded like I was giving him an out—making that first date our last date because of my messed up past—he looked me right in the eyes and assured me that my past did not matter at all to him. Music to my ears!

That immediately changed the whole dynamic of the evening. I no longer felt like I had to reveal all my shortcomings for his sake. And Ernest apparently overcame some uneasiness of his own because he began to talk more.

He told me he was an associate pastor and music director at Pastor Clint Brown's FaithWorld Church and would soon be ordained as a minister himself. He also informed me that he was the former music director for *Without Walls* and Paula White Ministries.

Was that why he'd appeared so uneasy at the beginning of our date? I wondered. *Did he think I would shy away from him once I learned about his calling?*

In fact, it did catch me off guard, and for an absurd moment, I thought, There's *no way I could be a minister's wife!* To my utter surprise, I had begun to size up the situation in a marital context. *How would we look hand-in-hand as Mr. and Mrs.? How would his last name sound with my first name?*

I erased those thoughts just as quickly as they arose and resigned myself to just enjoying Ernest's company. No long-term commitments, no premature planning of where this was headed.

Ernest and I laughed and talked for hours on that first date once the initial weirdness wore off. As much as I attempted to dispel thoughts of long-term commitment, the most beautiful sensation that night derived from a "knowing" in both our hearts that that date represented only the first of many more wonderful dates to come.

༄༅༅

That following week, I was back in the saddle in Chicago, beginning my third season as *Ebony Fashion Fair's* commentator. Rodney also returned for his fourth year with the show. We became like two peas in a pod. I could talk to him about anything—anything that is, except Ricky and Ernest.

News about my breakup with Ricky had spread through the crew long before we were back on tour, so by that time, everyone (that is, everyone with tact) knew to avoid that topic around me. Rodney especially chose to avoid all talk of Ricky. He'd never liked the idea of us being together in the first place. "Ricky just isn't good enough for you, Jada," he'd told me a number of times.

I didn't tell Rodney about Ernest because he would surely tell me I was jumping into another relationship too soon. Rodney and my other over-protective friends—like Princess and Dereka—would believe I had acted rashly in falling for him. Well, what *is* sensible anyway? And who gets to decide what it is?

My life felt different with Ernest, like I uncovered a gem I'd found in no other person. *Refreshing, loving* and *promising* described Ernest best. Wouldn't it be sensible to be attracted to someone like that?

I didn't want to defend my position when telling anyone about him. They would only doom me to hear things like "It's too soon," "You hardly know him!" and "*Another* long-distance relationship?" I didn't want to hear those things, nor did I want to believe they could be right. So, I kept Ernest a secret.

Ricky had used our separations as a reason to complain and an excuse to do whatever he wanted. As a result, long-distance relationships were taboo in my mind. However, as the months went on, Ernest and I talked on the phone for hours at a time and visited each other as schedules permitted. And yes, it didn't escape me that I was in yet another long-distance relationship.

Fortunately, in delightful contrast to Ricky, Ernest used our distance in a positive way. To him, it meant time to concentrate on his ministry and an opportunity to build up excitement and anticipation for our next scheduled date. That made me so comfortable with my traveling. It also made it clear that distance had not been the real culprit in my relationship with Ricky.

Years earlier, I'd set out to accomplish the goal of virginity until marriage and had made good on it until I met Ricky. I know now that what I lacked then, in order to meet that goal, was the passion, the conviction in my heart for the ways of God. I resembled the double-minded man that the Book of James in the Bible speaks of. I took a stand for what was right until the temptation became too great. Then I wobbled like a bowl of Jell-O. That is anything but pleasing to God.

But no more wobbling and wavering now! My heart was established in Christ. With the Spirit of Christ leading me and with Ernest in my corner, non-wavering would be an easy thing, right? Wrong! In fact, the backsliding of many new Christian converts stems from the misunderstanding that living right—according to God's commandments—becomes a cakewalk if you only dedicate your life to God. Not so. In fact, because one has resigned to living right, more temptations and trials come their way (compliments of Satan, not God), to test what they are really made of.

I was certainly not exempt from those trials because Ricky suddenly returned to the scene, begging me to come back to him. Sometimes it had seemed as if he didn't want me when he had me; but now that I had moved on, he was there pleading for a "do over."

"How pathetic of him," you may say. Do you know what's even more pathetic than that? The fact that I actually *did* consider Ricky's offer! I actually found myself torn between going back to a wretched life (but one that was comfortably familiar), or moving forward into beautiful, enchanting, but uncertain territory. Seems like a no-brainer, but not to the one in the decision-making seat. Many battered and abused wives and girlfriends remain entangled in unsafe relationships due to that same demonic spirit of familiarity: better the devil you know than the devil you don't know.

My solution? Prayer. In fact, over a four-month period, I prayed and prayed and studied God's Word. Finally, the strength to move forward with God came. The strength to go all out for God and not give in to my flesh felt good to me. A brand new, positive life had begun for me! A life that would include Ernest.

In spite of my decision, no one knew about Ernest yet. They didn't know because I didn't tell them. I didn't tell them because I didn't know how.

They would not understand—not Mom, not my mother, not my siblings; not my friends; especially not Rodney, who saw up close how I'd struggled through my previous relationship.

And then there was me. I really wasn't sure I knew what I was doing. Was it the right decision for me to get involved with another man so soon after my break-up? I didn't need my friends and family telling me what I already knew. Their responses would make me waver, and I didn't want to waver. So I waited—waited until I knew for sure what I really felt toward this wonderfully sweet, spiritually mature, boyishly handsome man.

Ernest certainly gave me ample opportunities to figure out what I felt as he called me every day, sometimes three to five times a day. No matter what occupied his attention at that moment, he took the time to let me know he was thinking about me. While traveling with his band, he called. Going to rehearsal, he called. Leaving rehearsal, he called. Going to church, he called. Leaving church, he called. I fell in love with the attention, as much as I did with the man, himself. He made me feel good all around.

Most of all, Ernest loved me for me. Not because of my glamorous career in fashion. Not because he could pick up a magazine at the checkout counter and see my face. He loved me for my laugh, for my outgoing personality, for my Godly love and for my inner beauty. Because of all my good points, and in spite of my faults, Ernest loved the *real* Jada, not the *model* Jada.

After my previous relationship, I had a revelation of my own: A man cannot and will not define who I am. I am who God designed me to be and no one can define me better than the One who created me. I believe that many women find themselves attempting to discover meaning for their lives through the man in their lives. This is a wrong-headed idea and sometimes, we have to find that out the hard way.

On New Year's Eve 2002, Ernest and I pledged a life-long commitment to each other. Then in February 2003, six months after we first met, Ernest asked me to marry him. Saying "yes" came easy.

Having to now tell everyone about him was not so easy.

꧁꧂

I first broke the news to my mother, BJ. I called her in Tennessee and, after exchanging pleasantries, began apologizing to her for not taking her advice when she warned me about moving in with Ricky. I apologized for being stubborn and misguided. I proceeded with how my breakup from him occurred. "Why didn't you tell me you were going through all that?" my mother chided. "You should not have been dealing with that alone!"

She continued to listen intently and sympathetically, trying to take the blame for my bad relational decisions, being a poor example for me by staying with my father through so much turmoil. I never wanted her to carry that guilt; I had to learn that it was not all of her fault. We cried through our apologies, confessions and acknowledgments. We both felt relieved, having talked through everything.

I then told her that I'd made the ultimate promise to God to follow His ways and how, almost immediately afterwards, He sent the most wonderful man to me. I quickly recapped for my mother our six-month long heavenly relationship, with marriage as the pinnacle.

"When are you planning to get married?" she asked with excitement in every word.

"Uh, next week at the Orlando courthouse," I answered hesitantly, knowing that was yet another big shock for her to absorb.

"What?" she shrieked. "You can't deprive us of a wedding!"

"Well, with me being on the road and with no time to plan a wedding, Ernest and I agreed that going to a Justice of the Peace was just fine. The important thing is that we'll be married."

"You will have a wedding. Don't you worry 'bout a thing. I'll take care of it all."

After hanging up the phone from that conversation, I immediately called Ernest—too excited to contain the news about what my mother said for another minute. I asked his opinion about a wedding. He could hear my excitement and concluded that whatever I wanted was fine; he just wanted me to be happy. Another reason I loved him so much.

Ernest picked the date of June 7, 2003, and the wedding plans began.

BE-You-TIFUL
TRINITY

Live, Laugh & Love
PRACTICAL APPLICATION

I believe that many women attempt to find meaning in their lives through the men in their lives. This is a wrong-headed idea that many of us have had to debunk the hard way. I can't tell you how often I found myself seeking validation through the men in my life when clearly I should have been seeking the Kingdom of Heaven. That is where my true validation comes from.

When I met my husband, I had a treasure chest filled with ideas about what a man should be and what he should mean to me. Some of those ideas were good and some of them were stained with the bitterness of my past. I was blessed to find a man who was willing to take time to understand my past and work through it with me.

Though my man wasn't as "perfect" as I expected him to be, I had to realize that my expectations of a fairy tale Prince Charming were just that: a fairy tale. Conversely, I had a set of equally fantastic negative expectations that were just as damaging and unrealistic: I suspected every man of being an ogre. I almost missed out on the best thing that ever happened to me because every time I looked at Ernest, I saw Ricky or my dad. This was a curse I had to take responsibility for and change with the help of God.

They say you can't look backward and move forward at the same time. Whoever "they" are, they're right. You have to let go of the past and let God bless you with the gifts of your future. *What's done is done.*

Be-You-Tiful Live, Laugh & Love Tips

I have learned three powerful lessons in life. It's from these lessons that I offer this "trinity" of advice.

1. **Live** each day with thanksgiving because every moment is precious.
2. **Laugh** whether you are happy, sad or indifferent. Laughter is like medicine.
3. **Love** with every fiber of your being (even when you're not loved back). That's unconditional love…God's love.

Why should you "believe" in this trinity? Here are my answers:

1. Why live?

We are alive because of God's love and grace. Many people who go through life unaware of God's grace don't think there's much to live for. If you're one of those people, try being more thoughtful about and aware of what you have in your life. I can almost guarantee that will make you more thankful.

God did not give us this precious gift of life just to experience suffering. Sure, we all have to go through some tough situations in life, but only a grateful heart will experience the fullness of life. I mentioned earlier in the book about not wanting to live anymore, but it's funny how, even when we're little children, God strengthens us through our purpose. My purpose back then was to live and watch over my little sister.

2. Why laugh?

If you could only see the real "villain" behind most of your problems in life, you'd burst out laughing—too often, it's *you*. The Bible clearly says that there is a time to be born, a time to die, a time to plant, a time to reap, a time to kill, a time to heal, a time to break down, a time to build up, a time to weep and a time to laugh (Ecclesiastes 3:1-8).

That's right. It's scriptural: there's a time to kick back, let your hair down and have a crazy, loud, out-of-control laugh every now and then. Laugh at life, laugh at nothing, but most of all, laugh at yourself. *Then move on.*

3. Why love?

Love is the foundation for long life, real joy and laughter. You can't really live and have an abundance of happiness and joy without participating in God's love. The neglect and lack of love in my family when I was growing up contributed very little to my knowledge of love. It contributed only to my intimate knowledge of neglect and abuse.

How can a little child know that he or she is not being loved? The truth is we are created out of love so we're already familiar with it. We expect it to be part of our environment because it's supposed to be part of our environment. When it's not there, we miss it.

When we focus our attention on abuse and other negative forces, we cut ourselves off from that love even more. We can be two steps away from love and not see it because we're focusing on the ways in which we've been hurt.

Take your mind off your pain and look for the love that might be standing just over there.

Start walking—find your way back to love.

CHAPTER SEVENTEEN

Planning Ahead

LOOKING BACK TO MY WEDDING and the events leading up to that day, it still amazes me to think about how it all came together, despite my hectic schedule. The genuine desire by so many people to ensure that we enjoyed a superb wedding day overwhelmed me. One thing I learned for sure: it takes a whole village to have a successful wedding! Even today, I am moved with tears of gratitude when reminded of what it took to bring about that magical moment. From beginning to end, my wedding played out as a fairy tale come true, thanks to so many loved ones!

As soon as I publicized our marriage plans, offers to help poured in from everywhere. My aunts, uncles, cousins and extended family in California all stood by ready to jump in with any task handed their way. My *Ebony Fashion Fair* family and some FaithWorld Church members pledged their assistance as well.

By this time, Mom, my mother and my siblings were already knee-deep in planning details, since my mother spread the news to them almost immediately after hanging up from our life-changing, heart-to-heart phone conversation. With my blessings, they handled everything from researching hotel and airline rates to ordering and sending out invitations.

Being on tour did have its advantages. It gave me the fortunate opportunity to select flowers and color schemes, dresses and shoes from various boutiques, specialty shops and department stores around the United States. Between shows, the models and I spent numerous hours creating bridesmaids' bouquets and ushers' corsages over giggles and girl-talk sessions.

With Jackie—my wardrobe-assistant-turned-bridesmaid—and Rodney, the search was on for the perfect wedding dress. Our hunt ended successfully at a privately owned bridal salon in Atlanta.

I spotted the dress hanging and sensed it to be "the one" even before slipping it on. I anxiously wiggled into it and it hugged every curve of my body. Staring in the mirror at myself with that dress gave me the assurance that it definitely was the one. I had that exquisite, eggshell white, strapless, beaded gown from the couture collection of designer Stephen Yearick immediately shipped to my home. I breathed a huge sigh of relief with that major task under my belt.

※

One Sunday, during the final month of our 2002-2003 season, we performed at the Marriott City Center in Denver. Afterward, most of us attended a party held in one of the suites on the top floor of the hotel. A spectacular view of the Rocky Mountains offered the perfect backdrop for such a sophisticated crowd. Everybody who was anybody in Denver graced us with their presence.

I stayed at that party much longer than I wanted to. As commentator, I am the spokesperson for the models—a role that I am humbled by and, therefore, do not take lightly. As soon as I mingled, smiled, shook hands and talked shop (long enough not to seem rude), I snuck away to my room. My wardrobe assistant had even commented a little earlier that I looked weary and should perhaps retire for the night.

Weariness was a common state for me in those days. Almost every free moment in between show times somehow evolved into "wedding planning time." Whether I was shopping around for something or on the phone confirming details with my mother, my time was not my own. I'm not complaining, though; I boasted the title of World's Happiest Bride-to-be!

I'd no more than entered my room, kicked off my shoes and headed toward the bathroom to start removing my makeup when the phone rang. I glanced at the clock. *Oh brother, who could this be?* Ernest and I had spoken on the phone in between the show and party, so I wasn't expecting to hear from him again. Unless, of course, he just wanted to tell me again how much he missed me. I smiled at the thought.

I answered the phone sweetly, expecting in return that soft, gentle voice of my soon-to-be husband. Instead, I got an earful of loud commotion in the background with a frantic voice close to the mouthpiece, forcing out the word, "Help!"

"Who is this? What's wrong?" I yelled into the phone, frustrated by my own confusion.

Someone else then got on the line and spoke with more clarity. "Jada, come to room 2021! The models are fighting! Hurry—2021!" *Click*.

I couldn't make out the voices, but then again, I didn't think about it long enough to try and figure it out. I grabbed my room key and charged out the door in stocking-clad feet, suddenly forgetting how tired I was.

Right outside my door stood one of my bridesmaids, Tiesha. She said she saw me leaving the party and decided to come check on me. I quickly filled her in on the bizarre phone call and we both took off running down the hall for the elevator.

As we approached the elevator, Tinika, another bridesmaid, came running from the stairwell, yelling, "Jada, you have to come upstairs. Two of the girls are fighting."

At this point, anger arose. Mainly because of the models behaving like children, but also because I was, once again, called on to play mediator. From age six, or perhaps even earlier, I mediated for my mother and father. Then there was the fight about Candace's diary that I'd ended up in the middle of several years ago.

As we walked briskly down the corridor to room 2021, my anger turned to embarrassment as I realized the fight took place right next door to the party suite! *All those upscale, high-society people must've heard all that ruckus! How insensitive and immature can these models be?*

Tinika talked the whole way up, filling us in on what sparked the argument. Finally we approached the room; however, not a single bit of noise could be heard. *Thank goodness,* I thought. *Maybe they came to their senses and everything's settled.*

The door stood ajar so we walked in, with me leading the way. Consumed by my anger, I never stopped to consider why the lights were off. Out of habit, I just reached for the switch on the wall. Just as I flicked on the lights, there erupted the loudest chorus of "SURPRISE!" that I'd ever heard.

I jumped back with what must have been the funniest, shocked look on my face because many of the surprise attackers broke out in hysterical laughter. It took a moment or two for my heart to stop racing. They got me good!

As my eyes scanned the room, I burst into tears. Every corner bloomed with beautiful seasonal flowers. Colorful streamers and balloons hung festively from the ceiling. Obviously much time, attention—and most importantly, love—went into the planning of it all.

How did they do all this without me noticing? I stood in awe at their efforts, but especially at the people who stood there smiling at me—my friends, co-workers, tour managers and even some of the partygoers from next door. The love expressed by those people in that room that night blesses me to this day.

Then there were the gifts. Oh my, so many gifts filled the room that I couldn't imagine how I would open them all in one night. *Just how did they bring all these into the hotel without me seeing anything?* Big packages, little packages—all meticulously wrapped. Funny, but I never even thought about the gift-receiving aspect of getting married. Just being with Ernest for the rest of my life was gift enough.

Running off to the courthouse to get married would not have allowed me moments like this. Boy, was I glad my mother talked me out of that.

The gifts were great, but the cards attached to the gifts truly represented the highlight of the whole bridal shower.

One card read: *Jada, I haven't known you for long, but I am glad that I do know you. You have been an inspiration to me in my walk with God and I just want to thank you. Your life has been an example to me of how to live a godly life. Thank you for your encouragement and thank you for being a wonderful boss.*

Another one stated: *Jada, I never knew about Christianity before, but I am so thankful to have learned about it from having you show me a better way of living. Congratulations to you and Ernest.*

Again and again, through card after card, their words of gratitude were great testimonies of how God had used (and continues to use) an ordinary person like me to touch the lives of so many. I did not have to give up the modeling career I dearly loved and go into a pulpit in order to generate positive change in people; I just had to be obedient to His calling right where I was.

At that moment, a light bulb lit in my mind and I understood that the whole purpose of me dedicating my life to Christ was the good that would come to *others'* lives through me, not just the benefits to my own. That foundational truth allows my life—as well as the lives of all Christians—to resemble the unselfish life of Christ, Himself. What joy I felt, having that all revealed to me through simple gift cards!

🔅

Just a few weeks after that bridal shower, my plane landed in Orlando and I mentally "took off running" in the final planning stage of my big day. I was the working definition of a nervous wreck!

One would think that years as a runway model and commentator—facing stressful deadlines and last-minute changes on a regular basis—would have prepared me for a simple wedding. Not so. Mainly because two maids of honor, two best men, eight bridesmaids, eight groomsmen, two ring bearers, ushers, hostesses and a couple hundred guests do not a simple wedding make. It wasn't "simple," but it wasn't elaborate either—I wanted my wedding to be stylish, memorable and comfortably enjoyable for all.

At times, though, I imagined my wedding as the most splendid, exquisite fashion show ever held: *As each member of the wedding party promenades down the aisle, a gentle, feminine yet commanding voice describes their outfit to the seated guests. Later, I confidently stride down the long, silk-covered aisle to the "oohs" and "aahs" of the crowd as they stand in respect of the grand finale piece: a stunning, eggshell white, strapless, floor-length Stephen Yearick wedding gown, embellished with beads. The voice announces every detail of my outfit for the engrossed crowd, including how it hugs every curve of my body down to my knees, where an appliqué in the back introduces a magnificent, two and a half foot long, fishtail train. My bun hairdo is partially covered with an off-the-face veil, featuring an assemblage of pearlized beads draped across my forehead. I am carrying a beautiful, cascading bouquet of fresh mauve, pink and white orchids, brilliantly capping my stunning ensemble.*

I gracefully extend my opera-length gloved hand to my debonair and handsome groom, who awaits his bride at the altar. Adorned in a black, Sean John four-button suit with coordinating mauve-colored tie and handkerchief, he gallantly receives me as his lover for life. That same sweet and powerful voice comes out of nowhere, declaring us Mr. and Mrs. Collins.

Now, *that* is a bridal processional! Why not have a little fun with it and create in my mind the fairy-tale-perfect wedding that every bride-to-be hopes for?

🔅

Thursday morning: back to Orlando International Airport to pick up the remaining female members of the bridal party. It was great to see them all—some, such as Princess and my sister, I had not seen in almost a year. We hugged and babbled excitedly while gathering bags. We then headed to the hotel for everyone to freshen up for lunch.

After a full week of planning, organizing, purchasing and creating things, we most certainly welcomed a day of fun. Dereka arranged a bridal party luncheon for the bridesmaids, maids of honor, hostesses and I at a fancy restaurant at Universal Studios. We ate, laughed and reminisced. I handed out thank-you gifts, prepared by my sister Rece, which represented only a small token of my enormous appreciation.

Our leisure time was shortened by the daunting reality that a whole list of things still needed attention. In those remaining forty-eight hours, the reception hall got decorated; the flowers, cake and menorah were delivered; the rehearsal conducted and rehearsal dinner enjoyed. I wish I could say the tasks were completed without a hitch, but that, unfortunately, was anything but the truth.

A wrong catering date (due to miscommunication) and a late delivery of flowers and candles (due to a company emergency) caused me to break my personal vow to remain cool no matter what. Last-minute fires I had to put out forced me to excuse myself and run to Ernest at the recording studio to keep from crying hysterically in front of everyone else.

Like magic, Ernest had only to hold me in his arms and whisper soothingly, "Don't worry 'bout a thing; everything will work out," to make it all okay.

The flowers, cake and candles did make it in time, despite the florist's medical emergency that previously interrupted their family business' scheduled delivery. To correct the catering fiasco, my mother politely recruited some members from the church to help serve the food that she so proficiently managed to secure from a different source. In fact, my entire wedding crew, as well as family members, chipped in courteously, allowing all deadlines to be met. The beauty of it all rested in the fact that none of the wedding guests could tell major glitches had occurred.

Problems always have a way of ironing themselves out, and thank goodness my pre-wedding mishaps were no exception. However, with God in my heart and Ernest in my corner, I could rejoice in my spirit, even in the midst of those problems.

BE-You-TIFUL
TRINITY

Murphy's Law
PRACTICAL APPLICATION

When I was younger, I heard it said, "Whatever can go wrong will…that's Murphy's Law." I learned that life is filled with unpleasant situations and circumstances that will either teach and build you or frustrate and break you. We all learn from our failures, disappointments and frustrations, whether we choose to or not. The issue is *what* we learn.

Do we learn to be bitter or do we learn to be better?

We can't predict our future, but God has given us the assurance that all things work together for the good of those who love Him.

I always had the perfect wedding planned (in my head). *Everything* would be "perfect"—from the flowers to the bridesmaids. But fate brought about its own version of "perfect" that didn't quite match the spectacular event I'd envisioned from girlhood. Although the caterers didn't show and the menu had to be pieced together by my family, though the reception hall was decorated at the last minute by family and friends and my dad was not there, everyone around me thought it was wonderful, beautiful…perfect.

In the midst of the wedding breakdowns, I learned a valuable lesson: life is what you make of it and perseverance is a weapon against opposition. I had a choice to make, either to crumble under self-made pressure or to just go enjoy the moment. I chose to enjoy it.

"What Can Go Wrong Will" Tips

Many times, we find ourselves pulling out our hair under the pressure of our own expectations. When we do this, we rob ourselves of the right climate for peace and joy.

This affirmative trinity is about handling things going wrong.

1. Know that things happen.

To live life without expectation of things going wrong is just plain foolish. There will always be roadblocks to the accomplishment of your goals and those roadblocks can cause disappointment or hurt.

One way to avoid hurt when you have setbacks is to never set up another human being as your only means of achieving a goal. You can't forget the frailty of human hands and human plans. When human beings are involved, everything that can go wrong will go wrong, but there is one sure Hand that awaits to give you comfort and aid if you only ask and acknowledge Him.

2. Prepare for the unexpected—have contingency plans.

If you don't expect some adversity in life, you'll be blind-sided by it when it happens. Just because you can't see something coming doesn't mean you shouldn't and can't prepare for it. Always have a backup plan. Remember God had one for us: Jesus Christ. Also, don't be so prideful that you can't see God's helping hand showing you a way out of your difficulties. Pride can cut you off from God's guidance and that makes you a target for failure.

3. Live in the moment and enjoy everyday life.

Someone once asked me: "Where do you live?" I answered with a little sarcasm: "In my mind."

This is a fact. Our street address is not where we really spend most of our time; the place we live is in our minds. Most of us reside at Stressful State Street while some of us live on Joyful Moments Avenue.

Here is something you can do every day without anyone noticing. When you feel really stressed out, go and put on some relaxing music and take yourself on a little miniature mental vacation in your mind and enjoy the moment.

Remember: *Life is a gift God made for us, so live it and enjoy it.*

CHAPTER EIGHTEEN

Mr. & Mrs.

JUNE 7, 2003. THAT MUCH-ANTICIPATED DAY finally arrived! Though thunderstorms threatened, I woke knowing it would be the most wonderful day of my life. My entourage and I arrived at the church at noon for the two o'clock ceremony. Being a stickler for promptness, I made it quite clear to the wedding party that the ceremony would start on time.

Before I went up to the dressing rooms, I snooped around the church, giving everything one last look. I stood in the doorway of the reception hall, marveling at the amazing transformation that had taken place in mere hours. My mother rounded up some help and, in the absence of professional caterers, they busied themselves overseeing the arrival of huge pots of food. I said a quick prayer, thanking God that my mother so masterfully saved the day after finding out that the caterers had us scheduled for the wrong date. Since it was too late to hire another company, Momma simply organized an epic potluck.

I tiptoed away so I wouldn't disturb them and visited the splendid sanctuary. Seeing Mom's visions become reality absolutely took my breath away. A sea of pink, mauve, lilac and burgundy flowers, bows and ribbons adorned the aisle, the altar and the beautifully crafted archway on the dais. I gave it all my nod of approval, then hurried up to the dressing room to get ready.

I decided to relax as much as possible that day—whatever happened, happened. I popped in my favorite gospel CD and sat down at the vanity to apply my makeup. Moments later, someone knocked on the door. I figured the bridesmaids were finished getting ready and came to see if I needed assistance.

I cracked the door slightly and peeked out. When I saw the smiling faces of my Aunt Dolores and my grandmother, I screamed in excitement. Tears flowed. The doors to the bridesmaids' dressing rooms flew open and, in seconds, everyone was drawn into the "hug fest."

Aunt Dolores, who had played benefactor to both Rece and me for as long as we could remember and hosts her annual dinner for the *Ebony Fashion Fair* to this day, had contributed financially to my wedding. It wasn't until almost a year later that I learned how much. Dolores just gives and gives and gives, never asking for anything in return—which is why she is so blessed.

Seeing my grandmother was bittersweet. I shed tears of happiness to see her; tears of sadness at the reminder that I would not see Grandpa. It had been twelve years since my grandfather went to Heaven, but it still hurt to know he would not be walking through the door behind her. My mind flashed back to the many wonderful talks he and I had as he drove me back and forth to piano lessons.

My grandfather always gave me an uplifting word, especially at times when I could not figure out what I wanted to be in life. He told me I would be the prettiest model in the world if that was what I wanted to be. He told me I would be the smartest broadcaster in the world if that was what I wanted to be. He told me I would be the most entertaining talk show host in the world if that was what I wanted to be. On June 7, 2003, I just wanted to be the happiest bride in the world—I know my grandfather smiled from Heaven with his approval of that as well.

⚜

As two o'clock neared, my heart danced faster with each glance at the clock. Soon, Mom, Rece and all the bridesmaids congregated in my dressing room for one last check before lining up for the processional. Christie whizzed about, proficiently organizing us all at the top of the stairs in preparation for the processional.

One by one, we would descend the stairs to be paired up with our escorts who waited at the double doors to the sanctuary in the foyer below.

As we stood there, each anticipating her turn, I peered through a window that overlooked the sanctuary. The crowd, the bright lights and studio cameras all took my breath away. That was when it hit me: *This is really it!*

Daryl, Ernest's older brother, and Gloria, a long-time Collins family friend, stepped onto the dais. Daryl took his place at the piano and Gloria magnificently rendered a soulful version of "I Believe in You and Me" by Whitney Houston. Next, my cousin Tina from California recited a beautiful, heartfelt poem that she'd written especially for us. Last, but not least, the soft but powerfully melodious voice of Ernest's sister, Rhonda, filled the auditorium with Stevie Wonder's "Ribbon in the Sky."

As the last song ended, Pastor Doug and Ernest walked out from behind the choir stand and took their places. My heart fluttered ecstatically when I saw Ernest and realized how soon he would be my husband.

The processional was elegant—the wedding party entered the church two-by-two. Christie came to the top of the stairs to help me down to where my god-brother, Jonathan, waited to escort me down the aisle. Thank God for that—my legs had inconveniently turned into spaghetti noodles!

The spotlight turned to the double doors behind which I stood with a huge grin and watery eyes. I thought of my father. He wasn't there on my special day, despite an invitation. I told myself his absence was a good thing—best not to chance another confrontation like the one at my aunt's house several years ago.

When, as a girl, I rehearsed my wedding day in my mind, it was my father who escorted me down the aisle. In that fantasy, he was a sober, loving man, beaming proudly as he walked beside his precious little girl. Years later, I came to realize that those fairy tale images of my father would never be reality. Yet no matter how much I hated the things he did to us, deep down inside I still wanted him to be there.

The double doors opened wide. The music started. My wobbly knees stiffened. We proceeded to the altar with grace and confidence. I recalled that runway scene I previously envisioned for this moment. With cameras flashing, I nodded and smiled at everyone as I passed by.

What made that divine stroll all the more extraordinary was the music: "I Will Love You Always," an original song written and played by Ernest, especially for me. If the words of Ernest's song were what guided me to the altar, it was Jonathan's assistance that got me up the steps in my mermaid-shaped dress. (Important safety tip to every bride-to-be: always practice going up and down the stairs in your gown *before* the big day!)

Finally, Ernest and I stood hand-in-hand under the flowery arch. Oblivious to the crowd and the wedding party, we gazed into each other's eyes, repeating after Pastor Doug our vows to love, honor and cherish 'til death do us part. Before saluting me as his bride, Ernest once again perched himself on the piano bench to serenade me, this time with the song "You Are So Beautiful to Me." While he sang, the large screens positioned on either side of the platform allowed me to glance at the crowd. There wasn't a dry eye in the place.

Amid all the joyous tears—thanks to the most moving nuptials I could have ever asked for—the culmination of our ten-month courtship presented to the world a beaming Mr. and Mrs. Ernest Collins, Jr.!

Princess' words, spoken to me years ago in my astonishment over a six hundred dollar bottle of wine, came back to me now: "This is how we roll!"

࿇

The most memorable and funniest scene occurred with the tossing of the bouquet. It's a bizarre tradition, when you stop to think about it. Bouquet tossing—with its roots in England—has for centuries been the most anticipated wedding reception event for the single female guests. As custom has it, catching the bouquet means that the good fortune of the bride in marrying is passed on to the recipient. Despite a complete lack of statistical support, whenever a bride prepares to airmail her flowers, single women turn into wide-receivers and free safeties. The women at my wedding reception were no exception.

As I raised my bouquet hand, a transformation occurred that caught me off guard. Sophisticated models-turned-bridesmaids—swank women so many of Ernest's male friends and relatives had been agog to meet—dove for that coveted prize as if it was a fumbled football. One model's leap was so spectacular and zealous that her shoe went one way while her corsage went another. She landed on her fanny in the center of the floor. Ending up an ungainly heap in front of an audience didn't phase her one bit—she accomplished her goal and snagged a piece of the bouquet.

As the day's events drew to a close, the skies opened and the rain came down. It was as if God, through that downpour, had opened the windows of Heaven showering blessings upon all. As Ernest and I stepped into our new life together, I knew that because each of us was complete in God as an individual, our marriage would be complete as well. In that rainstorm, I saw the blessings that would overflow our lives into the lives of others.

As Ernest and I drove off to begin our life together, I reflected on my past, marveled at my present life and thanked God for His grace that carried me from there to here. Those old rags of oppression, depression, unworthiness and guilt were shed, making way for the eternal riches that exist through the new birth, making me as pure as a white wedding dress, as complete as the circle of a wedding ring and more worthy than the most expensive diamond set into that ring.

⚜

With my wedding day behind me and an amazing life in front of me, I realized how God revealed portions of the big picture to me as I made myself ready to receive them. I truly believe that for each and every one of us, God has a unique plan and purpose grander than we could ever comprehend. However, to save us from ourselves, I think God's plans and rewards are revealed in proportion to our level of faith and readiness. More faith, more revelation. More readiness, more ability to carry out the plan.

I was now ready.

BE-You-TIFUL
TRINITY

Love & Marriage

Here's a trio of thoughts I've come to on love and marriage.

1. It's worth the wait.

There is no hidden secret to obtaining the gifts of wisdom and love. Like any good father, God has unselfishly given us His plan for prosperous living. Through His son Jesus Christ, He has graciously given us access to prosperity. He promises us that, if only we will seek it from Him, He will not withhold any good thing.

One would think that knowing this would be enough to secure our hearts, but our prideful nature short-circuits our belief system by insisting that we do things *our* way. We're like desperate treasure hunters in search of something that's hidden in plain sight: love. We look for it through our physical cravings and are continually surprised when we fail to find it there.

What is it they say: insanity is when you do the same thing over and over again, expecting different results?

You want love? Go to the Source. God is love, so doesn't it make sense to look there first?

2. The purpose of the union.

It wasn't until after I got married that I truly understood the purpose and purity of two people joining together into a Holy union. Although I knew that God brought my husband and I together for His design and purpose, I continued to try to live in a fairy tale love story. I envisioned this handsome Prince Charming coming to rescue me, sweeping me off my feet, loving me, living with me happily ever after. It didn't help matters that I lived most of my youth devoid of love and happiness. I had absolutely no idea what I was daydreaming about.

As I matured and began knowing God a little better, I awakened from my daydream to reality. From the wedding plans to the altar, from moving in together to the arguments, this fairy tale princess had to learn humility, trust and the real meaning of the word *union*.

3. God's protection plan.

Alas, some of us show up on our wedding day with the wrong intentions. Our thoughts are focused on *us*, not our partner and not the union. I think we need to re-direct our thinking. We shouldn't show up on the wedding day to join hands in holy matrimony without knowing God's purpose for the union.

Love has mercy on ignorance, and that's a good thing because if it weren't for God's mercy, I would have ended up with the wrong man, probably given birth to a child, possibly ending up with a nasty divorce, making a complete mess of my life.

Pride and love doesn't mix. Love makes problems easier to bear; pride makes them unbearable. "Love," the Apostle Paul says in 1 Corinthians 13:4, "is patient, love is kind. It does not envy, it does not boast, it is not proud." Through pride, I was in a dark place for a long time before I resubmitted my heart and recommitted my life back to Jesus Christ.

We see so many bad examples of relationships and marriages today. There are these so-called Hollywood marriages that seem to run parallel to the roles these people play on the big screen. The marriages, like the movie roles, are fictitious and provide momentary entertainment for a few. The idea of a lifetime commitment seems not to figure in these very public unions at all.

God has given us a perfect example of commitment through His Son, Jesus. He lived and died for us, promising never to leave us nor forsake us. That's what I call real security and protection. What commitment does God ask of us in return for that sacrifice? Not much—only our love and obedience.

CHAPTER NINETEEN

Resolutions

ONE DAY, SHORTLY AFTER MY WEDDING, I SAT AT the dinner table gazing out of the window, mulling over the events of my wedding day. I was angry at my father—angry because someone at the wedding had asked why he didn't give me away. The question caught me off guard and embarrassed me. Certainly, I was used to his absence; so to me, that day would progress as any other day without him. But to have the issue exposed to hundreds of people—most of whom didn't know my history with my father—created a deep disturbance in me that I wasn't prepared for.

I needed to face this anger; perhaps even reason through it. I wanted to finally deal with my feelings for Daddy. It was time.

So, I began to ask myself questions. Foremost in my mind: *Why was I embarrassed by my father's absence?* I realized I was afraid people would judge *me* negatively. Their perception of me would be less than perfect. Worse yet, maybe the embarrassment resulted from my own harsh perception of myself. I'd wanted desperately to be something other than a rejected child who'd made good. I'd wanted a mother and father who loved each other, and a nice home where I could feel safe and protected. I'd wanted that fairy tale life, but it seemed far from me.

I never discussed my family issues with my friends—too painful a topic, I suppose. So, as I sat in my new apartment with my new husband, I realized the time had come for me to grow up and deal with the truth of my past—no matter how painful it was. Of course, over the ten-month period Ernest and I spent together before marriage, he learned a whole lot about me, about my childhood and even about Ricky; but this time the conversation would be very different. This time, not one dark corner of my soul would be spared in my determination to set my life on the right path, once and for all. I told Ernest EVERYTHING!

I loved my husband even more that day for the way he understood and cared. After I poured out my soul, he looked at me and quietly said, "You can't hate your father forever. He made some mistakes, but the only way you're going to be able to move on with your life is if you learn to forgive him and let go. You have to learn to love life and enjoy every moment as if it were your last."

I knew he was right. I knew I needed to let go of all of the bitterness and hatred that I'd built up against my father. Bitterness and hatred I'd justified as being righteous "dislike" of his actions. However, in order to heal, I needed to first and foremost reveal the truth. I did hate his actions, his character, his habits. I didn't know how to separate him, the person, from those actions and habits, which formed his character. Therefore, I hated the person as well.

From that moment forward, I began my mission to forgive my father and forget his trespasses against me. It wasn't easy at first because of my lifetime of blaming him for every bad event that had ever taken place in my life. I realized I'd really started on the path of forgiveness that summer in Boston when revelation after revelation came during my research for the TV production on low self-esteem. But the busyness of life kept me from really pressing through to a resolution with my father.

This time, a more mature and deeper heart-search revealed the very thing driving me to hate, to love, to succeed and to survive: fear! I was still driven by it! I'd evolved into a basket case of fear—afraid of losing; afraid of rejection; afraid of everything. My ultimate fear, though, was that of being hurt. I saw what my father had done to my mother and I swore to myself that I would never let that happen to me. Fear of being hurt restrained me from letting people all the way into my heart.

On the other hand, that fear drove me to be the best. I'd worked very hard to get to where I was, but I was unable to enjoy the process because of my motive. Fear told me I had to stay ahead of my competition. In reality, passion for my work would keep me just as far ahead of my competition, but in a much more enjoyable way. I needed to spend more time loving what I did and less time blaming others for the things I didn't have the opportunity to do.

One day, I got up enough nerve to call my father. I intended to really, really talk to him. I picked up the phone, dialed the number he had given me about a year ago and waited. While it rang, I wondered if it still worked, since I had never used it before. I expected someone to answer and tell me that I had the wrong number. After the fourth or fifth ring, I expected to hear an answering machine.

"Hello?" A man's voice answered. Dad!

I froze for a second, then felt relief as I really wanted to face my fears. "Hey, Daddy!" I said in as light-hearted a tone as I could muster.

"Who is this?" he inquired. I immediately remembered that he has six or seven children, so it was understandable that he wouldn't know right off which one I was.

"This is Jada," I told him.

"Hey, Baby!" he said with great enthusiasm.

At that moment, I swallowed my pride and asked for a few moments of his time to speak with him frankly. He agreed. I apologized for all of my negative feelings toward him and his new children. I asked for forgiveness and explained to him that we missed out on many years of our lives, but that we didn't have to miss out on any more.

During that conversation, I realized that I desperately missed my father. I wanted to re-establish a relationship with him and was willing to take whatever first steps were necessary. I told him how much I missed him at my wedding.

"I have a picture of you and your husband right here in front of me," he said.

"Really, which one?"

"Well, I don't know, but both of you have on white shirts."

I knew right away that it was one of the pictures taken during our pre-wedding festivities. It happened to be the same picture that Ernest and I have hanging in our living room.

Daddy said he wanted to meet my husband. That really got me excited and smiling. Suddenly, it occurred to me that we were talking like a normal father and daughter, which is all I'd ever wanted. Since childhood, I'd dreamed of a normal family with normal relationships.

When I asked about my younger half-brother and—sisters, he confided how much they looked up to me. Again, I felt compelled to apologize for my behavior. Then, a wonderful, but unexpected thing happened: He actually apologized to me for all of the pain he'd caused and confessed that he should have handled things differently. The only purpose of my call was for me to apologize to him; however, hearing him say how sorry he was worked wonders for my spirit!

In continuing our conversation, I learned the underlying factor to my father's pattern of abuse and self-destruction. As a result of his time spent in the Vietnam War, psychological injuries—depression, anxiety, paranoia, delusions, psychosis and even drug and alcohol abuse, overwhelmed his well-being. These symptoms were common in the men who served in that war. Even though my father escaped physical harm, many of his buddies did not, which was enough to add survivor guilt to his mental distress. It all certainly made me realize that unless I had walked in my father's shoes, I could no longer condemn him for his actions.

We can't go back and change anything, but we can take advantage of the remaining years of our lives. I now know that life is too short to hold a grudge. I love my father and I am glad that I have a second chance to be his little girl. I pray for him all the time.

⁂

In the days to come, my father and I would hold long conversations about our earlier years growing up in California. He even taught me a little bit of history about my paternal great-grandmother and great-grandfather, whom I never knew. My favorite story was about how my great-grandfather crossed the border from Texas into Mexico. While there, he married a petite, beautiful Mexican woman. In fact, my great-grandmother was so tiny that he hid her in a potato sack in order to sneak her into the United States in the back of an old pickup truck. I learned a lot from my father, and I enjoyed our conversations.

I had an opportunity to talk more with my mother as well—openly and honestly. It was a hot summer day in Orlando when my mother picked me up from the airport. I was excited to take the time off from my hectic fashion show schedule and photo shoots and wanted to finish my book. I had given the book to my mother to proofread and to give me some pointers. Remember, she graduated Valedictorian of her class.

I was glad to see her. She is as beautiful now as she was when she used to pick me up from grade school. Her skin is still radiant and her curvaceous body still turns heads. Not to mention her beautiful black wavy hair and her heart of gold.

I was afraid she'd be offended by my honesty after reading my book. I was more afraid because she knew how I really felt. We never talked about real issues. Other than the day my Dad left us, I had never seen my mother cry. It was as if she was terrified to let others see her weakness. Today would be different.

"I had a chance to finish your book," she said, "and I think it's really good."

There were a couple of areas that she felt I should modify and I took her ideas into consideration. "What do you think about the things that I said about Ann Lee?" I asked.

I hadn't really resolved in my heart if I should be so honest about resenting my grandmother so much. And then, she began to tell her story.

"Your grandmother loved you and all of her grandchildren. She just had a very difficult life. She would do anything for her children. I can remember how she would walk miles, even though she was crippled, to bring me my lunch." Tears were running down her face. "I was so embarrassed when I heard that thump at the classroom door. I knew it was Ann Lee bringing my lunch. I was embarrassed because she was crippled, you see," she added. The tears continued to flow.

My heart was breaking because I was embarrassed, too. But why?

"When her children ended up on drugs and in prison," she continued, "she had to become tough because of some of the things they would do to her. She wasn't always mean. She was a loving and caring lady until the disease overtook her body."

"What kind of disease was it?" I asked. After all these years, I still did not know.

"It was a form of leprosy," she answered.

I don't know much about leprosy other than what I read in the Bible, but I made a mental note to myself to study up on it later. I told my mother how mean Ann Lee was to us and how I thought she hated my sister and I, but loved my older male cousin who lived with her.

"She had to take care of him all of his life," she said. "There was a different kind of love and protection for him because he didn't have his mother around."

I guess I could understand that now, but back then it didn't make much sense. I told my mother for the first time in my life how I was sexually abused and fondled. I told her how I hated going to my grandmother's house because her live-in boyfriend would always touch me.

"I thought you and your sister were safe," she responded, tears pouring down her face. "I just didn't know."

On the way home, we talked about life, love and family-things neither one of us knew much about, except how much it all hurt.

My mother told me about how she met my father and how young they were when they got married. She pleaded with me not to hate him and to honor him before the Lord. I admired her for that. I took that as an opportunity to share with her how I had finally come to a place of forgiveness. So, I went back and re-read this book because I realized that it's not over. I still have time to make it right.

My advice to anyone who is still holding a grudge against a parent or other family member: Let it go! Life is so much better when we forgive.

BE-You-TIFUL
YOU

Just Be YOU
PRACTICAL APPLICATION

I spent so much time trying to be what others wanted me to be—trying to be like the beautiful people on TV—that I really didn't know who I was.

It seems I spent a lifetime attempting to come up with ways to fool others (and myself) into believing I was someone else. I pretended my way through life, trying to get others to accept the illusion I'd created for myself. I fooled some people some of the time and others none of the time.

The truth is that I wanted to be someone else because it seemed more glamorous, or more exciting...or less painful. However, when I stepped back to take a look at myself and my life, I was pretty glamorous and exciting in my own right!

We sometimes look at our lives through a magnifying glass that enlarges fear and intimidation. This kind of tight focus blurs our inner vision. Our individual unique abilities and qualities are gifts from God, and our focus on what we think we *ought* to be can cause those gifts to go unnoticed. Can you imagine not opening a gift given to you by a loved one? Why leave unopened gifts from the One who loves you better than you love yourself?

God put those abilities there for a reason. Be humble enough to ask Him to help you discover them and grant you the wisdom to properly develop and use them.

Remember: *Being ordinary is no challenge, so dare to be different.*

"Be-You" Test

What does it mean to "be you?" How can you tell if you're content with your own life? Answer the questions below honestly to find out.

1. Are you envious of other people's possessions and/or discontent with your own?
2. Do you always second-guess your own ideas?
3. Do you go out of your way to avoid confrontation?
4. Do you need approval from someone else to make a decision?
5. Do you find yourself making excuses for your appearance?
6. Are you trying too hard to fit in — and maybe feeling that you're not really succeeding?
7. Do you find it difficult to sincerely compliment someone else's success?
8. Do you have difficulty facing your failures and using them to succeed the next time?
9. Do you alter your views in the presence of certain people?
10. Do you compromise your values around people whose values are different from your own?

If you answered "yes" to more than half these questions, consider what it says about how content you are to be you, how sure you are of your own values and opinions and how comfortable you are in your own skin.

The first step on any journey is realizing that it's time to go. If you're not happy to just BE YOU now, it's time for you to take that first step on the road back to your true self.

EPILOGUE

Be-You-Tiful Treasures

trea-sure *noun*

1. wealth, especially in the form of jewels and precious objects, often accumulated or hoarded.
2. something of great value or worth.

Encarta® World English Dictionary © 1999 Microsoft Corporation. All rights reserved. Developed for Microsoft by Bloomsbury Publishing Plc.

I pray you've been encouraged by my testimony of how God has turned my pain into joy and my struggle into strength. If you are inspired in even a small way, then this labor of love will have been well worth the effort. I pray, too, that God's plan and purpose for your life may have a deeper meaning than what you've considered before.

Just "Be You!" I know, I know. Another cliché you've heard many times before. But it's more than that—it's a mandate for life. If you've tried living your life through other people, letting their opinions shape you, letting them cast you in whatever role they think you should play, then you should know that your success in life will only come from a sincere desire to succeed at being *you,* and not by playing the roles other people cast you in.

I have it on good authority that this is so. God assures us of success if our confidence lies in Him. Other people can help us, but they don't have the power to give us vision—that's Kingdom business.

When I decided to pursue my passion to be a model and a public speaker, I had no idea that God was laying the foundation for my real purpose. I thought I was building my career; God was building a ministry. As I developed a passion to help build and strengthen people, particularly women, I realized that my desire to become a model had put me right where God intended me to be. Life was no longer about what God had given me; it was about what *I* could *do* with what He'd given me. To paraphrase John F. Kennedy: *Ask not what God can do for you, ask what you can do for others.*

Now, you might think God wouldn't give someone a mission in a secular environment like the modeling industry, so full of sexuality and vanity. I don't mean to offend anyone, but not everybody meets God in church, nor does everyone who goes to church meet God. This is because some churches have become very secular indeed, and because God is not confined to four walls and padded pews.

I can't help but remember what Christ Jesus said when the Pharisees criticized Him for hanging out with tax collectors and prostitutes: *"I have not come to call the righteous, but sinners to repentance."* (Luke 5:32) When they attacked Him for not keeping the Sabbath as *they* thought it should be kept, He replied, *"The Sabbath was **made** for man, not man for the Sabbath."* (Mark 2:27)

In my secular environment, I was able to affect the lives of those with whom I worked every day. Every one of us can do that; we're given the power to go into the world and not be of the world. How else are we to win souls for the Kingdom if not by upholding God's standards and values wherever we live and work? That's true ministry, I think—when we can be effective wherever God places us.

I believe the people God wants to reach are all over the world in places most "religious" people wouldn't think of going. If we want to help Him reach them, we can't rub shoulders only with other believers—that's just preaching to the choir, and we know what Jesus had to say about that. In fact, I believe we all have a ministry, but we don't all look at life with ministry in mind.

So ask yourself this question, "Can I serve a need beyond my own?" That's what true ministry is. That's the very image of God and that's why you're here.

✧

Here's another Big Question for you: *What's your self-image, and who are you trying to please?* The Scriptures say we're created in God's image, so it seems to me it's *His* image we ought to reflect and His opinion we should care about.

Do you believe your life is useless or that you don't have what it takes to be what you think you should be? Time to turn a deaf ear to that kind of negativity. Your soul—your spirit—is God's creation; you better believe He created it without mistakes.

God's purpose for your life lies in the *true passions* of your true *self.* So what are you passionate about? When you get a handle on that, you get a glimpse of that little spark of the divine in you—that little reflection of God's image.

God has positioned us all to be productive individuals in society. As long as the Earth endures, there will be problems to solve, inventions to be dreamed, sicknesses to cure, hunger to be fed. As long as people exist, there will be homes to build, children to teach, paintings to paint, books to write, songs to sing. So find out what you're passionate about and get busy with your purpose. Whatever it is, God has already placed a fire in your heart for it, but it's up to you to fan that flame 'til it takes hold.

And don't give up if it seems weird or impractical. If we all were passionate about the same things, only one type of thing would ever get accomplished...and the world would be a truly dull place.

Jesus says, *"Ask and it will be given to you; seek and you will find, knock and the door will be opened to you."* (Matthew 7:7) That's a promise. A covenant. We knock, He promises to open the door. But we *do* have to knock.

✧

The thing that lifted me up was the recognition of what was truly me—that image of God within me. The thing that almost destroyed me was *fear.*

Some people call it *insecurity* or *low self-esteem. I* used to think of it that way. But I've come to the conclusion more recently that these are secular, therapist-speak terms used by people who are still dealing with the *symptoms* of the disease and not getting down to the *cause* and the *cure.*

In order to deal with what the world calls insecurity and low self-esteem, you must identify these things for what they really are: spiritual ailments. You can't cure spiritual ailments with worldly medicine. The medicine needed for this kind of sickness is different.

If we're unaware that our true self is that divine image in which we were created, the *self* we are *esteeming* is a mere shell—a frail and mistake-prone physical self. If we apply a salve called *self-esteem* to that shell, *we're not treating the part of us that's really sick*. We can't cure fear with shallow human methods that fail to take our spiritual reality into account. That merely treats the symptoms, not the disease that causes them. Fear must be rooted out spiritually, not just covered up with therapeutic band-aids.

Fear is a serious disease and I see people every day who use their celebrity, popularity, influence or affluence to make it seem that they are the picture of health while inside they are full of fear. I think it's a tragedy that we don't realize how often we give the devil a platform through snake oil salesmen who talk about real issues from their place on the "world stage," but who can't give real hope because they don't acknowledge the spirit.

Fear and hopelessness make it hard for us to trust in anyone, even God. But God doesn't want us to live in fear and hopelessness. Scripture says He has not given us the spirit of fear but of love and a sound mind—a mind He expects us to *use*—to know Him, know our true selves and know what will lead us to the heights of fulfillment or the depths of loss.

The key is *knowledge*—the all-encompassing knowledge of God, not the limited knowledge of man. As we learn more about our world, ourselves and our universe, we mistake our sheer wealth of material knowledge for wisdom. But it isn't wisdom if it leaves out the most important factor: the reality of the human spirit.

The thing I dislike most about modeling can be summed up in the words "competition" and "comparison." *Comparison* tempts us to judge ourselves against others, which requires that we first judge others—something God frowns upon. *Competition* turns our fellow human beings into adversaries and causes us to envy them. Both of these things tempt us to exalt ourselves above others when scripture says we should love our neighbors as we love ourselves and warns us against being selfish and self-exalting.

Again, it comes down to loving, not the shell but the image of God *within* the shell. I believe we must see that spark of God-given greatness in *all* of us and fan the fire of our love for one another *because* we see it. It's what Christ has commanded—yes, *commanded*—us to do: *"A new command I give you: Love one another. As I have loved you, so you must love one another."* (John 13:33-35)

That's real beauty.

what Christ has commanded—yes, *commanded*—us to do: *"A new command I give you: Love one another. As I have loved you, so you must love one another."* (John 13:33-35)

⚜

Every day, I get up and say, "I'm free." I speak my freedom into existence and I repeat this all day long because I believe that when we speak words, we speak things into existence; and the words that we speak shape our environment. We say so many useless and idle things in the course of a day that we don't realize how much power we have (and waste). The Bible says life and death are in the power of the tongue, so we should be careful what we give life to.

Not only did I speak those words into existence, but I also got a couple of prayer partners to help me. Now you may ask, *Is that necessary?* Well, picture going to a gym and trying to lift some weights off the rack, only to find that the weights are too heavy to lift by yourself. What do you do? You get a spotter to help you lift the weights.

I believe there's a message in everything, and the message from this physical reality—that you sometimes need help with life's "weights"—is simply that none of us were meant to handle life's pressures on our own. You need a spiritual spotter every now and then to help you lift. Don't be prideful, get a prayer partner and ask God to help you.

Remember this: Salvation is a *process*, and you shouldn't feel like a failure if you rise and fall. Besides, it's easier to fall when you have help to get back up.

⚜

My life was filled with negativity until I recognized that my true self was the image in which I was created—His image. You were created in that same image, but is that the image you're reflecting? Take a moment to look at your Self. Do you see God's image in your spiritual mirror, or do you see an image that's been crafted by yourself and others?

Jesus Christ said: *Be perfect, therefore, as your heavenly Father is perfect.* (Matthew 5:48) This isn't possible for our bodies or our minds, but for our souls—the part of us created in His image—it's a can-do.

BE-You-TIFUL
PHILOSOPHY

Seven Attributes of Beauty

1. ACCEPTANCE - We must learn to accept that we are just the way God created us.

2. FAITH - We must believe in the power of God and in the purpose for which He created us.

3. ACTION - Faith without works is dead. We must have determination to take action—to follow through on our belief in God's purpose for our lives.

4. COURAGE - We need courage to step out with faith.

5. HOPE - Hope is the heartbeat of Purpose. Hope gives us the drive to pursue our destiny.

6. RESPECT - We must respect our Creator and His choice in how He created us. We have to respect others based on who God created them to be. And last but not least, we must respect ourselves.

7. LOVE - God is love. He created us based on His unconditional love. We must learn to love God, love others and love ourselves.

Jada and Ernest
Collins pictured on
their Wedding Day

Jada and Ernest Collins Wedding Party

Jada and Ernest Collins Wedding Party

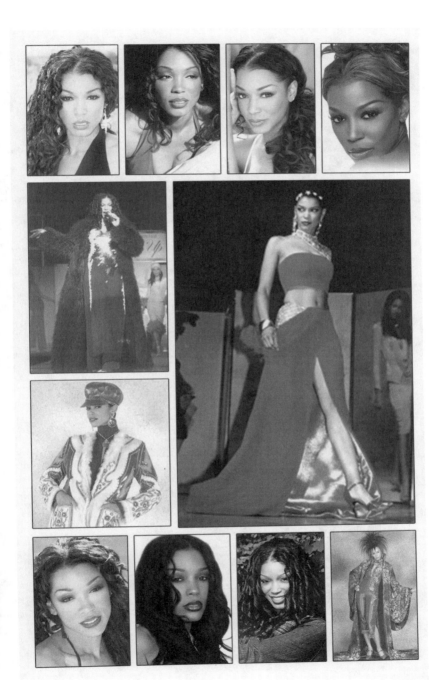

Jada Collins commentating at the Ebony Fashion Fair.

REFLECTIONS

Ebony's impact on Black America...

Ebony's impact on me

WHILE WORKING WITH SOME OF THE MOST talented African-American men and women ever, I realized that I was a part of something larger than life. I was no longer on the outside looking in through those glossy pages; yet, what I became a part of proved bigger than my imagination. When you work for the number one black-owned and -operated publishing company in the world, each day's involvement counts toward history.

Over the past sixty years, Mr. John H. Johnson, founder and chairman of the Johnson Publishing Company, his wife, Eunice W. Johnson and their daughter, Linda Johnson Rice, have built an African-American empire right in the middle of white America, by delivering news and entertainment to our community. In the '50s and '60s, while blacks endured segregation in restaurants, public transportation, schools, politics and any place else that symbolized the great American dream, *Ebony* plowed its way through that demoralizing system, giving our people a sense of pride, a sense of self-worth.

Acting as a social adhesive, *Ebony* empowered the African-American community with knowledge—knowledge of their brothers and sisters' challenges and accomplishments throughout the country.

We were a nation on the rise, and *Ebony* played an enormous role in the development of our history in this country. For the first time, we could see ourselves in print. For the first time, we could witness our issues being addressed. For the first time, our voices stretched across the nation. We were powerful. We were intelligent. We were black and we were proud.

As I walk the hallways in the Chicago headquarters, I relish the many historical *Jet* and *Ebony* magazine covers adorning the walls. On these covers are the famous stars and important political figures whose lives characterized the rise of black America. *Ebony* was right there to capture those moments.

Having graced the glossy pages of *Ebony*, *Jet* and covers of *Ebony Fashion Fair* magazines, I too have become a part of this history in print. Although I am proud to be an American, I am overwhelmed with pride to be African-American! I wouldn't change it for anything in the world.

At times I have had the amazing experience of working with Linda Johnson Rice, the firm's CEO. She's young, beautiful, smart, powerful and in charge of running the entire multi-million dollar operation. I once sat down to converse with Mrs. Rice, and within minutes I knew that I had come in contact with one of the most extraordinary black women on the face of this planet. I decided, right then and there, that I would be more than just a pretty face on a magazine cover. With the best role model available, I purposed in my heart to become an exceptional, twenty-first century businesswoman.

Thank you, *Ebony Fashion Fair!*

Thank you, Johnson family for inspiring me to

BE-You-TIFUL

ABOUT THE AUTHOR

Jada Collins

JADA COLLINS is the commentator and spokesmodel for the world's largest traveling fashion show, *Ebony Fashion Fair*. She joined the Johnson Publishing Company family in 1999 as an *Ebony Fashion Fair* model and then soon advanced to commentator and spokesmodel, as well as a face of Fashion Fair Cosmetics.

Jada has over one thousand fashion shows worldwide on her résumé. Traveling from San Francisco to New York to Rome and back, she has developed a love for fashion, life and people. She enthusiastically embraces her career, which places her among world- famous designers, models, actors and personalities.

Born in the San Francisco Bay area, Jada dreamed of a career in broadcasting and public speaking. Her early years were plagued with poverty, lack of confidence and other obstacles that threatened to hinder her dreams. However, at the age of twelve, standing at five feet eleven inches, she was pulled into the world of modeling.

When not traveling with the fashion show, Jada enjoys encouraging young girls and women across the country to do their best, love themselves, and reach for higher heights. She is currently laying the foundation for a TV talk show as part of her goal to enter the world of multi-media communications, where she can minister to young girls and women on a broader scale.

In 2003, Jada married gospel artist and minister Ernest Collins, Jr. Together, while residing in the Orlando, Florida area, they are building upon their strong Christian foundation to impact the world with a powerful message of hope through fashion, music, dance and ministry.

ALSO BY JADA COLLINS

BOOKS
Visit **www.jadacollinsonline.com** to order

Be-You-Tiful: The Threefold Process to Becoming You
10 Laws for being Be-You-Tiful
Be-You!: Positive Thinking for Today's Woman
Be-You!: Make-up Laws 101
J.C.: The Second Coming
Be-You!: Diva Versus Princess

MUSIC CD's
Visit **www.jadacollinsonline.com** to order

Poetic Truth by Ernest and Jada Collins
I Know a Man by Ernest Collins